The Honest Guide on Postpartum for New Moms

Conquer Guilt, Loneliness and Sleep Deprivation to Rediscover Your Inner Strength and Embrace the Joy of Motherhood

Alicia Filippone

Ash and Stone Publishing

CONTENTS

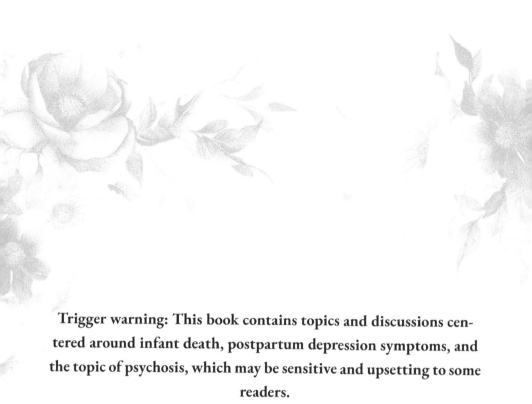

Trigger warning: This book contains topics and discussions centered around infant death, postpartum depression symptoms, and the topic of psychosis, which may be sensitive and upsetting to some readers.

INTRODUCTION

"Clean the house." Check! "Prepare and feed the baby." Check! "Get some daily self-care done." Check! "Exercise gentle parenting at every given moment." Check! "Engage with the baby throughout the day." Check! "Juggle the situation even when I know I need help." Check! "Quit my job so I can be a *better* mom." Check! "Follow the motherhood manual so I know everything is correct." Check! "Love every moment of the experience." Check!

Already feeling like you're the *only* mother who doesn't seem to have all her ducks in a row? Well, I'm happy to let you know that you, I, and every other first-time mother out there long to find this superwoman and ask her the one question we all have on our minds every hour of the day: "How does she do it?"

Meet Stacy. She's a 23-year-old first-time mother who lives with her significant other. Stacy has two older siblings who both have children of their own. Stacy would spend her free weekends babysitting and supporting her siblings in the best way possible with chores, school projects, and engaging activities. However, Stacy now has a child of her own to look after. She was confident she'd find her postpartum phase easy since she'd gained a lot of experience helping out her siblings with their children. However, since giving birth, Stacy is continuously pushing her physical and mental limits by thinking she needs to do it all since taking care of her nieces and nephews was a walk in the park. To her, new moms are in control of their postpartum journeys; therefore, playing weak isn't an option for her. So, Stacy is navigating her way through motherhood by trying to be superwoman, not accepting any weaknesses, and faking it until she makes it.

Now, let's go on to meet Hannah. She's a 28-year-old stay-at-home mother who's just had her first baby. Hannah is married, but because her husband works exceptionally hard to provide for their family in every way possible, he's hardly ever home to help her with the new baby. Ever since the birth of her baby, Hannah's been feeling drained, overwhelmed, and unable to commit to any of her household chores. Whenever Hannah suggests hiring help to her husband, he chooses not to take her seriously since she seemingly "sits around doing nothing all day." As it stands, Hannah's loneliness, exhaustion, and unstable thoughts are causing her to dread anything that concerns the upkeep of her baby, self, and home. On top of that, she's struggling to find the right support because she constantly feels judged and that she's overreacting and just being lazy.

Lastly, meet Debby. She's a 33-year-old career woman who recently had a baby and is now co-parenting with the father of her child. Debby is committed to embracing her new journey; however, because she values independence and ensures that everything concerning her is under her control, she's constantly "stretching herself thin." Debby has developed a lot of guilt over the first few months of being a new mom, even though she works tirelessly to ensure she and her baby are cared for. Now that she and the father of her child are no longer together, Debby is committed to getting her old body back so she can regain her confidence and possibly find a new relationship. So, as an outsider looking in, it's safe to say that Debby seems to have it all together. To the rest of us, she has everything any woman could wish for and always strives for perfection. However, nobody knows about Debby's internal challenges in working through her roller coaster of negative thoughts and emotions as she constantly compares herself to others.

Truth Is Key to All Postpartum Journeys

Journeys like motherhood can be humbling in the sense that no amount of on-the-job training, time, or provision can carry you through it entirely. Over the years, I've learned that all postpartum journeys require you to eliminate all possible expectations you may have in order to thrive, do it all, and have it all. It's about embracing motherhood in all its forms while creating a unique experience independently of what's *expected* of you, what others think, or what you imagined everything to be like. Here, truth is key.

Because all people and all children are different, you must understand that every motherhood journey will be unique. Our resources, mental spaces, support systems, priorities, commitments, and backgrounds are all different. Therefore, every story will be different. Granted, we may come together as mothers and share common struggles, thoughts, and surprises; however, no two stories will be the same. The one thing that remains consistent among all of us is that we strive to be the best versions of ourselves, so we're able to be the best moms we can be.

I Know Your Pain Firsthand

Motherhood is a very dynamic journey that's influenced and affected by several factors. So, there's no right or wrong way of going about it. However, in having us all share our everyday experiences while living our unique and individual lives, there's a comfort in knowing that those judgments and guilt come naturally to us all. Although we have diverse backgrounds, our pain, concerns, illnesses, thoughts, desires, insecurities, fantasies, and comfort zones remain the same. Therefore, in uncovering everything I'll share with you in this book, I'd like you to know that I do understand your pain.

In choosing to seek help and find solutions on your postpartum journey, I already know you're in a position of trying to make sense of everything at the moment. Have you ever played a game called tug-of-war? The game entails two teams pulling on opposite ends of a rope to see which team can drag the other over the central line. I believe tug-of-war is very similar to any mother's postpartum journey simply because there's this constant war taking place within you, where you're continually assigned the task of needing to figure out and understand your new self—and this completely new human being who's entirely dependent on you—and where you're headed from this point on. So you're constantly being pulled from one end of the central line to the other simply trying to get the *right* team to win, yet there's no exact manual on how to go about this. You're just winging it the whole way.

At this point, all you're looking for is a point of reference—a point, quote, message, or guide that makes enough sense for you to confidently take a stand and move forward. By finding even the most generic plan of action, you can gradually find your personal way forward by re-centering yourself and finding strength in your new journey. So, by finding your point of reference, you can put an end to your internal conflict and work toward achieving every one of the goals you have for yourself.

Why *This* Book?

I'm a 32-year-old stay-at-home mother who had my baby less than a year ago. While juggling a full-time job, household, newborn baby, and additional commitments, I've found my postpartum journey to be rather lonely and misunderstood. Even with adequate support and financial planning, I've found it increasingly concerning to realize that, while we may go out of our way to put plans in motion to prepare for our new arrivals, there's just something genuinely crippling about the internal battle we experience right after giving birth.

Being a new mom should be an amazing experience, right? I mean, it's a time to celebrate your new creation, grow your family, and take on a new role. However, just weeks into the journey, you already find yourself dreading everything, hating yourself, filled with complete negativity, drained, overwhelmed, weak, unprepared, guilty, emotional, and lost. Honestly speaking, it can be a mess.

I choose to open up to you and own my truth this way because I believe that it's empathy, compassion, vulnerability, and honesty that make us relatable. Nobody is looking for the perfect answers. Instead, we're simply looking for practical and effective ways to make it through this journey in one piece. So, by providing you with a comprehensive, practical, and supportive guide on how to navigate your way through the postpartum period, you'll complete this book feeling empowered and motivated to face your journey head-on. I'm putting all my cards on the table to help you see that change *is* possible, and that motherhood *can* be an enjoyable experience when it's handled in a healthy, balanced, and intentional way.

I want to prove to you that you're not a victim of your new journey and that being a woman isn't a punishment. To do this, I've structured this book to introduce a SMART approach that any new mother can use to achieve greater peace of mind, confidence, and personal resilience. I've been using this approach throughout my postpartum journey, and I can confidently say it's truly changed my life. Therefore, in sharing my experiences, foundation, and knowledge with other new mothers, I'm hoping it will leave you feeling as liberated and motivated as I did.

Chapter One

Mommy Matters and Postpartum Self-Care

I wanna sleep. I wanna eat. I wanna take a shower. I mean, before she wakes up, we gotta do this all over again.

Rachel from Friends

When you imagine yourself and everyone else you care about as a cup, you realize it becomes impossible to pour into the cups of those you care about when your own cup happens to be running dry or empty. You can only pour into someone else's cup if you already have something to give. Most people leave it at that and afford themselves the break they hope will refill their cup; unfortunately, time alone will not do this.

To make sense of it, I need you to think about what fills your cup. Your cup is made up of everything you bring to the table. This could be your skills and experience in your workplace, the emotional support you provide to family members, the financial support you offer to close friends, and the companionship you give to your spouse. So, whether it's checking up on your parents every week, visiting a close friend in hospital after their accident, supporting your spouse through the loss of a loved one, or providing your expertise on a work project, your efforts and input make you valuable to others because you've managed to establish relationships that allow others to rely on you.

So, let's say your cup is made up of skills, expertise, support, financial flexibility, and companionship. You need to understand that none of these ingredients came to you as an inheritance. From a young age, you cultivated habits, characteristics, hobbies, and skills that led you to be who you are today. And with those habits, characteristics, hobbies, and skills, you can impact those around you positively. Have you ever heard the saying, "Hurt people hurt people"? Well, just as wounded people go out of their way to break down others, those who empower others also go out of their way to motivate and inspire the people around them. Therefore, when your cup is made up of positive, uplifting, inspiring, and admirable qualities, you can share that with everyone else around you.

Helping and encouraging others can be very fulfilling; however, many of us make the mistake of concerning ourselves so much about those around us that we don't have enough time to check in on ourselves. When you find yourself giving and giving and giving, similar to what happens when you pour little portions of your cup out, you lose bits and pieces of yourself. And by not ensuring that you pour back into yourself after each occasion when you've been pouring into someone else, you don't realize that you're losing more of yourself over time.

Key Self-Care Habits Every First-Time Mom Should Adopt

Like the different dishes, fragrances, and hobbies we all favor, everyone will define what they deem self-care differently. So, while you may regard long walks, always having your nails done, and yoga as self-care, someone else may feel otherwise.

Among the many things you can do to take care of yourself physically, mentally, and emotionally, there are some important habits that every postpartum mother should adopt. Whether you already have a list of things you enjoy doing for yourself or need help figuring out where exactly to begin, here are key self-care habits you should always prioritize.

Getting Enough Sleep

Newborn babies are said to generally spend 12 to 16 hours of the day sleeping (*Typical Sleep Behaviour (1) – Newborns 0 to 3 Months*, n.d.). Before birth, the news that your little one would spend more than half the day asleep would have had you thinking, *Wow! This means I'll have a lot of time on my hands to attend to other things*, or *Wow! Motherhood doesn't sound too bad after all*. But, soon enough, you find yourself turning into a cliché right after birth when you start thinking, *Man, I hardly have time to do anything these days*.

Granted, newborn babies spend most of their day asleep. However, because they don't know the difference between day and night, you can be required to attend to their needs at any time. Most adults generally don't mind going a few days without getting proper sleep; however, this ability doesn't last for too long. This is because our bodies have natural internal clocks that are controlled by a part of the brain known as the suprachiasmatic nucleus (SCN) (*Sleep/Wake Cycles*, n.d.). The SCN uses our senses, specifically sight, to detect what part of the day it is; that is, our optic nerves detect morning and evening light. When this happens, the SCN instructs the body to release hormones like cortisol, which signal our bodies to wake up at the sight of light. Then, when it's nighttime, our optic nerves detect darkness, signaling the SCN to release hormones like melatonin, which prepare our bodies to feel tired and want to go to sleep.

As we get older, we train our bodies on when it's time to sleep and how many hours we should spend sleeping. So, the moment we start losing sleep during our postpartum journey, this causes an imbalance in our bodies; we are fighting our natural hormones to stay awake when we're supposed to be sleeping and go to sleep when we're supposed to be awake. Over time, this affects the quality of our sleep, leading to issues such as insomnia, sudden night sweats, snoring, restless leg syndrome, obstructive sleep apnea, and many other sleep issues (Harris, 2023).

When caring for your newborn baby, it's unfortunate that you can't feed, burp, or change your baby in a way that allows you to see them through the night. Attending to their needs is something you'll have to be on call for any time of the day and night. This makes it increasingly difficult for any new mother to get a solid night's sleep.

Did you know that a restless baby isn't entirely to blame for keeping you up at night? Other reasons can contribute to first-time mothers having difficulty sleeping during their postpartum period. That's because, after birth, our bodies go through many changes that make resting a relatively challenging thing to do. This includes

- the physical recovery process we go through during pregnancy, labor, and birth

- changes in our hormone and fluid levels, which ultimately affect our internal clocks that signal our bodies when to sleep and when to wake up

- a change in mood and appetite

- often finding ourselves not feeling tired or unable to stay asleep when nighttime arrives

- undergoing emotional and mental stress (Phillips, 2022)

Ensuring you get not only *enough* rest but *quality* rest is crucial. Spoiling yourself from time to time, having a bath each day, dressing well, and participating in any form of exercise are all great, but getting enough sleep is crucial to any mother. To help treat insomnia and improve your postpartum sleep, I've found the following habits to be a lot of help:

- Educating myself on sleep to understand how it works and what I can do to improve it as a first-time mother.

- Committing to a habit known as sleep hygiene, which involves devoting myself to practices like having a daytime routine, putting together a healthy sleeping environment, adjusting the light and temperature levels in my bedroom to suit my preferences, limiting my alcohol and caffeine intake, adopting regular mealtimes, and exercising regularly.

- Studying stimulus control, which taught me to use beds only for sleep and intimacy, set an alarm that trains me to wake up at the same time each day, and avoid staying in bed when I find it difficult to sleep.

- Consulting with a cognitive behavioral therapy for insomnia (CBT-I) practitioner, who helped recommend a healthy amount of time that I should spend in bed each night.

- Using intentional relaxation techniques focusing on meditation, controlled breathing, and other techniques that work on unwinding at night so I still have the desire to sleep even after waking up to attend to my baby during the night.

- Adjusting my sleep schedule so I'm able to sleep when my little one is also sleeping.

- Alternating responsibilities and workload with my partner, relatives, or close friends to afford myself enough time to sleep.

- Taking strolls and morning walks to recharge because exposure to sunlight helps realign my internal clock and gives me the desire to sleep when the evening arrives.

- Abstaining from consuming any alcohol, especially when I'm breastfeeding.

Occasionally, it may cross your mind to consider taking prescribed drugs, antidepressants, or over-the-counter sleep medications. In such cases, it's always advisable to speak to a doctor or medical professional who will consider the health of you and your little one before providing you with a way forward. This is especially important if you're breastfeeding.

Adopting a Healthy Diet

The importance of having a good and healthy diet during pregnancy also applies to the postpartum period that every new mom goes through. Usually, society places a lot of emphasis on encouraging breastfeeding mothers to eat well so their little ones can get the nutrition they need through breast milk. However, encouraging a healthy diet also applies to mothers who aren't breastfeeding. This is important to know because mothers who don't breastfeed tend to occasionally make poor lifestyle choices that they feel "only affect them." But, by taking something like diet for granted, you put your health and overall well-being at risk—and what good are you to your little one if you're unwell and not in a position to take care of them?

Postpartum nutrition is crucial because our bodies go through a lot before, during, and after birth. Carrying a growing baby inside you for roughly nine months, going through labor, and recovering from the experience all take a physical toll on the body. So, thanks to the already evident stretch marks, weight gain, saggy breasts, and other body changes, you're already not feeling your best. Aside from pointing out the overall benefits that come with having a healthy diet as a breastfeeding mother, nourishing your body after delivery means

- speeding up your recovery

- encouraging your body to produce milk

- supporting your overall well-being

Adopting a healthy diet doesn't mean curbing all unhealthy cravings and ignoring your sweet tooth entirely. Instead, it means ensuring that you eat enough and follow a diet that offers you all the nutrition you need. Now and then, you can use a bit of junk food and sweet treats to reward yourself on a planned cheat day.

It's important to monitor what you eat and the number of times you eat because there's a link between the postpartum period and emotional eating. This might be a secret shame to many mothers out there, like admitting to having a food obsession. Many new moms start to view food as a companion, relaxation method, or activity they run to when they feel bored, lonely, angry, stressed, or tired. Therefore, with no intentional effort to monitor your diet and make healthy lifestyle choices, you can find yourself unable to control the urge to eat.

I've learned that many of us don't always run away from adopting healthy diet plans on purpose. People often assume others don't opt for nutritious meals because "they're boring" and "aren't as wholesome as a hearty meal." However, most people aren't too obsessed about eating healthily all the time because they

- think it's expensive

- don't necessarily concern themselves about what they eat—they simply don't sit down and count all the calories, carbs, and nutrients in a meal

- believe most healthy meals don't include meat

- assume healthy eating means going vegan or vegetarian

- think they'll have to eat less

- think they'll have to have smaller portions

Healthy eating doesn't mean consuming salads meal after meal. It simply means ensuring the meals you eat contain enough nutritional value to benefit your body. So, in addition to a hearty stew or pasta dish, you could add some steamed vegetables to ensure your meal is nutritious. This is far from being anywhere close to starving yourself. Also, when it comes to believing healthy dishes are expensive, yes, certain products like organic options may be a little on the pricey side; still, a carrot remains a carrot whether you're getting it from an affordable or a high-end grocery store. You just need to ensure you read the packaging to find out how many nutrients you get from each serving.

"I hear you, Alicia, but where do I begin?" Many of us don't have the luxury of consulting a dietitian or nutritionist. So, here are the key guidelines I use to follow a healthy postpartum diet, stick to it, and benefit from it:

- A healthy and well-balanced postpartum diet must include a variety of carbohydrates like multicolored vegetables, fruits, and whole grains.

- A healthy and well-balanced postpartum diet needs to include a variety of proteins like seeds, poultry, nuts, and fish.

- Instead of opting for olive oil for cooking, use healthy oils including polyunsaturated fats, which you typically find in canola oils, grapeseed, and sunflower oil.

- Spend the first six weeks of your postpartum journey taking the prenatal vitamins you were taking while pregnant.

- Calories are essential in your postpartum diet; however, you should always avoid the processed carbs you typically find in cakes, candy, pies, and pastries, as they don't provide any nutritional value.

- Even if you aren't breastfeeding, try to avoid alcohol, as it's a source of empty calories.

- Try by all means to avoid fish that are high in mercury, especially if you're breastfeeding.

- Ensure you limit the amount of caffeine you consume.

- Make a consistent effort to monitor your weight.

- Stay hydrated by drinking a lot of water and sugar-free beverages.

- Avoid anything including peppermint, especially if you're breastfeeding.

- You can always increase your nutritious calorie intake to help your body produce more breast milk.

After giving birth, you should focus on repairing and recovering your body rather than losing weight. You can always try Mediterranean diet plans as a form of inspiration because they're balanced and ideal for maintaining your overall health and weight. But, if you have the means, you can always work with a nutritionist to help you develop a personalized meal plan that includes all the nutrients you need.

As a postpartum mother, foods you should always include in your diet include

- whole grains

- vegetables

- fruits

- lean protein sources

- healthy fats

- low-fat or no-fat dairy

In addition to having these foods in your diet, it's important to consider how you choose to prepare your meals. This means avoiding too much salt, sugar, and butter. Instead of frying your food, you can always boil, grill, or bake it as a healthier alternative.

Part of maintaining a healthy postpartum diet means ensuring you eat enough each day. Even if you have a big appetite, trying to squeeze all your calories into a single meal is never a good idea. Instead, it's best to break your meals into sensible portions that you can consume throughout the day. So, in addition to a light breakfast, lunch, and dinner, in between these meals, you can always include a nutritious snack such as fruits and nuts. A healthy diet plan can include as many as three snacks on top of breakfast, lunch, and dinner. And while you do this, remember to drink plenty of water. By following this diet plan, you're sure to be nutritionally satisfied and energized all day.

Remember that part of adopting a healthy diet means knowing how many vitamins and minerals you're getting during each serving. After birth, you lose a lot of nutrients; to help restore these, you should always ensure your diet includes

- collagen, to restore tissue in the body

- omega-3 fatty acids, which bring health to your brain and heart

- calcium, to build strong teeth and bones

- iron, to replace your blood hemoglobin levels

- iodine, to promote thyroid health

- choline, to promote brain health

- vitamin D, which promotes health in your bones and immune system

- vitamin B_{12}, if you don't consume animal products like dairy and cheese

Like any other healthy lifestyle decision, a good postpartum diet offers several benefits to mothers who've just given birth. This includes

- helping postpartum mothers heal

- encouraging and supporting breastfeeding mothers to lactate

- boosting energy

- helping mothers sleep

- helping mothers decrease the chances of suffering from postpartum depression

- helping mothers lose their postpartum weight in a healthy way

Exercising Regularly

The physical body you have now will likely differ from how it was before you got pregnant. And even with your second, third, or fourth pregnancy, the feeling will likely remain the same. Pregnancy introduces a lot of change and, while some women love their new bodies and intend to just "touch it up" through toning, others find it hard to accept their new bodies and may try their best to return to their previous physique.

Even with your healing and recovery from pregnancy and birth, you should be able to start exercising within the first few weeks of childbirth. Vigorous training isn't the only way to exercise to achieve results, so you should choose from an extensive list of different workouts. Everyone will have a different goal, but it's always a good idea to consider a few things before choosing which exercises and workouts you'll be going for. Pregnancy and birth complications, how you're recovering, and the type of birth you had will determine which options you can go for.

Top Postpartum Exercises Every Mom Should Try

Before beginning any exercise program, it's essential to ease yourself into it. This will help keep you healthy and able to achieve long-term success.

It's important to also remain realistic and patient in all your efforts because rushing your body won't help you in any way.

Before starting to spend up to an hour exercising at the gym, ease your way into things by practicing low-impact aerobic exercises first. You can do these for 20 to 30 minutes each day. Over time, and depending on how your body responds to the physical activity, you can add 10 minutes to your routine and include simple postpartum exercises as well. These additions can include exercises that work on strengthening your abdominal muscles and other body parts like your back, glutes, and legs.

If you find that a 20-minute workout is too much initially, scaling your routine down to 10 to 15 minutes can be just as good. To make your efforts a little more effective, you could consider including two workout sessions in a day that last 10 to 15 minutes per session. A good example would be going for a 15-minute walk first thing in the morning. Later in the day, you can do a 10-minute yoga workout for a daily total of 20 to 30 minutes of exercise. Both efforts will prove to be effective in the long run. Then, as you gain strength over time, you can increase the intensity and duration of your workouts.

When it comes to why postpartum exercise is good for you, there are numerous benefits that are worth considering. These include its ability to

- improve your mood

- increase your overall health

- tone and strengthen your muscles

- boost your energy

- support weight loss

- relieve stress

- encourage your body to sleep better

Postpartum mothers looking to "bounce back" may underestimate what light to moderate exercises can do, but I cannot stress enough how important it is to not push your body to the limit. As a first-time mom who may have a lot on her plate and is trying to enjoy even the slightest bit of self-care, committing to something practical and easy to do at home is key. Therefore, in that light, exercises worth trying include

- Kegels

- diaphragmatic breathing

- walking

- Swiss ball bird–dog holds

- cat–cow in tabletop

- Swiss ball glute bridge

- postpartum planks

- side plank leg lifts

How to Effectively Work Your Way Through Postpartum Exercising

Before beginning an exercise routine, assess how you feel, if there's any part of your body that still hurts, and how a workout would make you feel in terms of leaving you energized or exhausted.

If you happen to be experiencing any abdominal pain, vaginal bleeding, or discomfort in the pelvic area of your body, it may be a good idea to rest while you wait for your body to recover. Alternatively, you could speak to your doctor about your concerns in case you need a checkup or referral. Once you have the go-ahead, you can ease your way into a postpartum exercise routine by following these steps:

1. Start slowly by breaking your routines into manageable sessions and only exercising on select days of the week.

2. Hold off on any heavy exercises until your vaginal bleeding stops.

3. Because exercise promotes weight loss, prioritize light to moderate exercises if you're breastfeeding.

4. Pay close attention to your pelvic floor, abdominal muscles, and joints during every workout.

5. Don't shy away from trying different types of postpartum exercises.

6. Keep yourself hydrated at all times.

7. Rest as much as you can.

Keeping Yourself Hydrated

Staying hydrated has several health benefits, which include preventing frequent headaches and improving your skin. Unfortunately, not everyone makes a habit of drinking water regularly; while you may have been able to get away with this before pregnancy, choosing to not drink as much water as you should will eventually lead you to dehydration during your postpartum journey. This will include experiencing episodes of overheating, sluggishness, regular headaches, and urine that appears dark and concentrated.

According to research, postpartum mothers should drink roughly 2.3 liters of water each day. This equates to approximately 8 to 12 glasses daily (*Keeping Hydrated during Pregnancy and the Postpartum Period*, n.d.). Mothers who have always prioritized hydrating themselves properly will most likely not have a problem continuing the habit. However, for mothers who haven't cultivated the habit of drinking water regularly, it may be helpful to consider establishing some sort of water-drinking routine.

Many of us are aware of the amazing benefits that come with drinking water regularly and staying hydrated; however, we may fall off the wagon shortly after establishing some sort of routine simply because of the dull and tasteless flavor that comes with drinking water. Like most people, I spent many years thinking that "spicing up" water with fruits or consuming other liquids like plain milk wouldn't prove to be as effective as drinking plain water. Fortunately, I was wrong. Of course, carbonated drinks and a cup of coffee won't necessarily work as well as plain water, but this doesn't mean all hope is lost. If you happen to find yourself unable to achieve the required water consumption by drinking just plain water, you can always try the following alternatives to keep yourself hydrated:

- adding fruits to plain water

- avoiding caffeine

- eating fruits and vegetables that include a high water content

- consuming milk, soup, tea, juice, or sparkling water as an added source of water

- ensuring you hydrate your body with nutritious liquids each time you feel thirsty

- monitoring your urine to ensure it remains light yellow or color-less at all times

- not exposing yourself to intense heat

- drinking more fluids before and during physical activity

- drinking water first thing in the morning

Especially if you are breastfeeding, you need to stay hydrated and drink as much fluid as possible but don't make the mistake of assuming your intake needs to always remain the same. You must monitor your body closely as temperature, health, activity levels, and climate can all contribute to how much fluid you'll need in a day. So, in the event of you needing more fluid, respond to that need immediately to avoid dehydration.

Fun Facts About Staying Hydrated

As I mentioned earlier, there are many things that need to be clarified about water intake, hydration, and where exactly you can look to get the fluid you need. So, after doing some experimenting of my own, here's what I came to learn during my postpartum journey:

- Both foods and liquids contribute to your water intake.

- Every beverage you consume will contribute to your fluid intake; however, plain water is always best, especially for hydration.

- The best way to tell if you're well hydrated is to monitor your urine, as a darker appearance may indicate that your body needs more water.

- Carrying or keeping water around you increases the likelihood of you consuming water more frequently.

- You can always use fruits, herbs, and vegetables to spice up your water with natural flavors; however, for the best results, it's always best to add your fresh ingredients to the water and place the flavored water in the fridge to make it refreshing and tasty.

- Adding flavored ice cubes with chopped herbs and fruits can also be a cool alternative worth trying.

- You can use carbonated water as a source of fluid.

- You can always pair cucumber, honeydew, pear, and watermelon with mint, lime, ginger, and rosemary, respectively, to achieve a fun flavor in your water.

- Fresh vegetables and fruits are mostly water, so you can consume them to stay hydrated while also getting the nutrients you need.

- You can always use the time you spend waiting for something or someone to drink some water.

- You're more likely to remember to drink water when you include it in your routine.

Another problem most mothers have is the need to go to the bathroom a lot when they drink more water. This may not be an issue when you're home the whole day, but, as an active and busy mother myself, I sometimes find it pretty impractical to dash from one public toilet to the next when I'm out running errands with a little one. For many years, I've encountered a lot of mothers who prefer putting their water intake off until later in the day. However, I recently learned that postpartum mothers do have options when it comes to sticking to their water-drinking routine, even on a busy day:

- **Drink more fluid first thing in the morning**: Unfortunately, choosing to drink your fluids way earlier in the morning won't guarantee any success in terms of sticking to your goals; however, one of the benefits that do come with drinking your fluids a lot earlier in the morning is that you'll at least get through those repetitive bathroom trips right before leaving the house.

- **Have fluids between meals and not with them**: Instead of drinking fluids with meals, drink them between meals, as this will help reduce the need to use the toilet when you're out and about. Avoiding eating while out and about will also cut down on the need for bathroom trips when you're away from home. The last thing you want to do is place any pressure on your bladder and stomach since they're still healing from having all your abdominal organs compressed during pregnancy. So, try to avoid instances that will have you needing to hold in your urine for a long time.

Improving Your Gut Health

One of the things you should prioritize on your postpartum self-care list is gut health. Before pregnancy, not a lot of people take the time to monitor their digestion since "our bodies do what they should," but as a mother who's just given birth to her bundle of joy, you need to be on the lookout for any digestive issues that could indicate a problem if left unattended.

After pregnancy, it's normal to find yourself experiencing digestive issues like constipation, excess gas, and an inability to control your bowel movements. So, as you try to recover from giving birth to your newborn baby, struggle with getting enough sleep, and experience tons of emotional stress, all these factors also affect your digestive system. Constipation and excess gas are one thing; however, when you're unable to control the bowel movements in your body, you run the risk of having your stools occasionally leak from your rectum without any warning.

A woman's digestive system usually slows down after birth. When your body doesn't have enough stomach acid or digestive enzymes to release nutrients and break food down, this causes digestive problems. Unfortunately, unlike your body, which is gradually healing itself, your digestive system likely won't change if you leave it unattended. This means you will face many issues concerning your gut health in the years to come, and with that comes the risk of your body not receiving the nutrients it needs to stay healthy since food isn't being broken down properly when it reaches your stomach. Even if you take supplements and eat well, this won't prove to be effective.

Also, not having enough stomach acid in your body means it won't be able to defend itself against viruses and bacteria. This is bad not only for your overall health but also for organs like the colon since there will be a significant imbalance between good and bad bacteria. When you couple this with stress, the fact that you aren't getting enough nutrients in your body means even your hormones will begin to be affected.

Remember the leaking stools we just touched on? Well, that's a condition known as fecal incontinence. Here, food that's partially or not digested travels through your body and reaches the small intestine, only to cause an intolerable reaction that leads your gut to leak. Once your digestive problems reach that point, you'll then be suffering from leaky gut syndrome. This is because our small intestines contain small gaps or "tight junctions" that instruct the body on what should and shouldn't enter it. But if your digestive system isn't operating as it should, it becomes inflamed and starts to leak, allowing all sorts of toxins to enter your body (McSweeney, 2023). Already got big eyes from reading this? Well, I was just as shocked as you are. Thankfully, there are ways you can help ensure your body heals and supports your postpartum gut.

Ways You Can Improve Your Postpartum Gut Health

If you're finding yourself unable to control your bowel movements, then it may be a good idea to speak to a doctor or healthcare professional. However, whether you're having no problems concerning your digestive system or are noticing a few unusual things about your overall gut health, here are some simple and effective things you can do to improve it:

- **Prioritize mindful eating**: Many of us think digestion begins the moment we place something in our mouths, but this is far from true because it actually begins in our brains. To help our bodies break food down the way they should, we need to be relaxed enough to focus on what we're eating and what our bodies are doing. The best way to do this would be to practice mindful eating by not eating while standing, on the go, or in a hurry. For the best results, we must be seated, calm, and intentional about our actions.

- **Cook foods well**: Avoid dry foods like french fries or foods that don't have any juices you can slow-cook them in. Instead, opt for stews, soups, broths, curries, and casseroles. Because our postpartum bodies don't have the stomach acid, enzymes, or energy to break food down the way they should, you can always support your digestive system by cooking foods well enough to have them break down on their own inside your body. This will increase the chances of your body releasing and collecting all the nutrients it should.

- **Eat your food warm**: Eating warm food isn't just beneficial to us in terms of taste. It's also great for helping our bodies conserve energy. Usually, when we eat warm or hot meals, we take a little longer to eat, chew, and swallow. These small bits of food help a lot in digestion since food is a lot easier to break down when it enters the body in smaller portions. This will allow your body the time it needs to absorb all the nutrients it requires; also, by not expending a lot of its strength trying to break down large chunks of food, your body can preserve its energy.

- **Buy local organic produce**: You can help your body heal and digest food the way it should by ensuring your diet is packed with proteins and fats that can help regulate your hormones. However, as you may know, not all produce is the same; therefore, you can reduce food toxins by ensuring you buy organic food and wash it thoroughly before cooking or eating it. By buying organic food, you're able to avoid the hormones and pesticides that usually harm our bodies. So, the fresher and more natural it is, the better.

- **Consider digestive aids**: You may not want to hear this, but bitter foods are usually great for digestion. This is because they contain enzymes and acids that help break foods down. So, just like a supplement you take once a day, you have the option to purchase bitter digestive aids as tinctures or consume a tea or juice that's bitter. Of course, you would need to take these about half an hour before a meal, but this will certainly help in getting the job done. To make your efforts more effective, you can even go as far as taking supplements that contain digestive enzymes. But, if you do this, you must ensure you're getting the fluids you need to stay hydrated. However, be careful not to drink your fluids while eating as this will dilute your stomach acid.

- **Don't take stress for granted**: When we think of stress, we usually limit it to mental health issues. However, stress also affects our digestive system since it's controlled by a nervous system connected to the brain. When we stress over something for too long, this alerts our brain to release a hormone that will delay our digestive process. So, like the times we find ourselves unable to eat because we're stressed or anxious about something, the brain has a similar effect on our digestive process.

When you find yourself constantly stressed and unable to process foods correctly, this destroys your gut health over time because waste is no longer traveling through your digestive system the way it should, which automatically creates toxins in your body. This will eventually affect your immune system, exposing you to all kinds of harmful pathogens that your body won't be able to fight off.

The Importance of Self-Care for Long-Term Well-Being

Self-care doesn't just revolve around spoiling yourself with expensive gifts and having a brief feel-good moment. For any postpartum journey, self-care will always mean a lot more than that. In life, your physical appearance and mental state go hand in hand. By not taking care of your physical body through exercise, practicing good hygiene, and eating well, your poor physical condition will begin to affect how you think and feel about yourself. And by not investing in your mental well-being, you won't invest in your physical body because you will lack the motivation, confidence, and self-esteem to do so.

In that light, because motherhood takes a toll on every aspect of your life with all the change that's taking place, you must invest in yourself as much as possible. In this way, you won't seek validation, credit, and approval from those around you. By not giving yourself the reward and recognition you need, you will automatically desire this from others. When you have those moments of feeling unappreciated, overworked, and not valued, this will only worsen your experience. Therefore, take it upon yourself to refill your cup; otherwise, you risk making it everyone else's responsibility. And by investing in yourself, you are responsible for rewarding yourself for all the hard work you're putting in to raise and nurture your little one.

Resources to Help Out

Here's a list of resources and apps that you can use to monitor your overall health.

- **Poppyseed Health**: Apple only

  - https://www.poppyseedhealth.com/

    - Health-care app

    - Free

    - Virtual consults (nurses, midwives, and lactation consultants)

    - Articles and videos on sleep, nutrition, exercise, and tracking baby growth

- **Real**: Apple and Android

  - https://www.join-real.com/

    - Health-care app

    - Monthly or annual subscription

    - Virtual consults (doctors, nurses, and lactation consultants on breastfeeding, mental health, and infant care)

- Articles and videos on sleep, nutrition, exercise, tracking baby growth, and support groups

- **Expectful**: Apple and Android

  - https://expectful.com/

    - Self-care app

    - Holistic care

    - Free

    - Meditation and mindfulness exercises that reduce stress, anxiety, and depression, tailored to pregnancy and postpartum stages

    - Library of sleep sounds and music, and community forum

- **Mysha**

  - https://myshapods.com/

    - Community building

    - Monthly membership

    - A community of parents sharing resources and tools with advice to get through pregnancy and parenthood

- **The Shine App**: Apple and Android

  - https://www.theshineapp.com/

- Self-care app

- Free

- Manage stress, anxiety, mindfulness, and mental health

- Motivational messages, meditations, and other self-improvement resources

- **Peanut**: Apple and Android

  - https://www.peanut-app.io/

    - Community app

    - Free

    - Connects you with other moms who live nearby; chat, write blogs, and form communities with like-minded people

    - Discusses fertility, pregnancy, motherhood, and menopause

- **Baby Tracker**: Apple and Android

  - http://android.babytrackers.com/

    - Baby tracker

    - Free

    - Tracks feedings, diapers, bottles, solid foods, and sleep or naptimes

- **Huckleberry**: Apple and Android

- https://huckleberrycare.com/

  - Baby tracker

  - Free

  - Tracks feedings and nursing, bottles, diapers, solid foods, and sleep/naptimes

  - Optimizes sleep/naptimes based on feeding and sleeping patterns, as well as the age of the baby

  - Syncs with multiple devices like that of your partner or nanny

  - Huckleberry Premium provides in-depth analysis straight from their experts

- **What to Expect**: Apple and Android

  - https://www.whattoexpect.com/

    - Pregnancy and baby app

    - Free

    - Helps you prepare for parenthood and guides you through your journey day by day and week by week

- **Back to You**: Apple and Android

  - https://www.thewonderweeks.com/

    - Postpartum recovery program

    - Free

- Physical and mental guides

- Insights into everything that physically and mentally changes after pregnancy

- Proven methods to heal your diastasis and prolapse

- Mommy-proof workouts at home

- Pelvic floor with the BTY-Kegel exercises

- **Glow Baby**: Apple and Android

  - no website

    - Baby tracker

    - Free

    - Baby's first year

    - Information on milestones—starting solids, feeding, sleeping through the night, growth spurts, and so on

    - There's also daily parenting tips

- **Sound Sleeper**: Apple and Android

  - https://www.soundsleeperapp.com/

    - White noise machine that will detect the baby crying and start playing soothing sounds

- **Milk Stash**: Apple only

  - no website

- App for exclusively pumping moms

- Tracks how much milk is pumped and stored (fridge/freezer)

- Tracks how much milk the baby consumes during the day

- **Aloe Bud**: Apple only

  - https://www.aloebud.app/

    - Reminders throughout the day to eat, drink water, socialize, and so on

- **Aetheria**: Apple only

  - Resource for outlining the symptoms and attributes of mental illnesses and disorders, to better understand yourself

    - Provides coping methods for the highs and lows during the day

- **Day one**: Apple and Android

  - https://dayoneapp.com/

    - Journaling app, encouraging you to put your thoughts and feelings down throughout the day

Next Steps

While this isn't a baby book focusing on everything baby, in the next chapter we'll cover some tips, hacks, and strategies to help you relax and feel confident that you're covering the basics.

Chapter Two

KNOWING YOUR BABY BASICS

You'll learn to lower your expectations about what you can accomplish in a day. Some days, it will be all you can do to keep a baby safe, warm, and fed, and that will be enough.

Unknown

N ow that you understand the importance of taking care of yourself, it's time we got into what you need to do to look after your little one. Before having children, we thought that baby basics meant ensuring we got the feeding, bathing, burping, sleeping, and diaper changing job done. The goal was simple—a baby will only give you problems when one of these things isn't being done properly, right? But when you actually start the job, you realize that the "baby basics" everyone had been talking about aren't as basic as you thought they would be.

Diaper rashes, skin allergies, sterilized bottles and toys, sleep positions, a clean environment, and breastfeeding techniques are some of the many concerns new mothers have in providing an attentive and responsive routine for their babies. In promoting your child's overall well-being and development, you learn that your new journey is more than just a role you take on to ensure your little one is physically taken care of. It's a nurturing and ever-changing journey that requires you to establish a personal language with your little one so you can dive into understanding, responding, and attending to every one of their physical, emotional, and mental needs. This means using this new language to communicate with them effectively through sounds, facial expressions, gestures, and body movements.

Having to engage and interact with a toothless somebody day and night can be both interesting and challenging. This is because a lot of the time, even after covering the physical basics, that simply isn't enough. Coupled with the crying that won't seem to improve anytime soon, you spend hours of your time playing an odd guessing game that requires you to comprehend a language that you've never heard before. After a bit of time doing trial and error, you may be lucky enough to figure out what the real problem is, but put on the wrong face, sing the wrong song, play the wrong game, or make the wrong move, and these little people will *not* shy away from expressing their wholehearted disapproval as your unhappy customer.

Your Newborn Baby Basics

Since "the customer is always right," it's important to know and adopt some basics that should set you up for the first two to three years of your child's development. Because situations that leave your baby extremely upset and emotional often make you feel like you don't know what you're doing, it's essential to understand basic baby care so you're confident in meeting, recognizing, and interpreting your baby's needs.

Bathing and Grooming

Baby grooming requires essentials like shampoo, a hairbrush, clippers, and a toothbrush. Apart from the hygienic aspect, baby grooming also comes with benefits that include keeping your baby clean and dirt free, lessening the chances of having your baby fall ill, and providing your baby with a comforting experience.

Baby grooming isn't as easy as placing your infant into an adult bathtub and giving them a quick bath. In addition to ensuring you're keeping your baby afloat and can support their neck and head, your baby's movements and irritability can make the experience a little challenging sometimes, especially when you're a first-time parent. Fortunately, there are some quick guidelines you can use to master the basics:

- To avoid drying out your baby's skin, limit your bathing sessions to three times a week.

- Use a sponge or cotton ball to clean your baby in the first three weeks after birth so you can monitor their umbilical cord stump.

- Before grooming, gather everything you need and place it nearby to avoid needing to leave your baby unattended.

- After undressing your baby, use a towel to keep them warm as you prepare to bathe them.

- Even when your baby isn't in the water, it's crucial not to take your eyes off your little one at any moment.

- Avoid placing your baby in water for the first few weeks following birth.

- To ensure you're using warm water to bathe your baby, place your elbow in the water to assess if there's a stinging sensation. If it stings, it's too hot.

- Instead of using soap to wash your baby's face, use a damp sponge, cotton ball, or cloth.

- While washing your baby, pay close attention to cleaning their neck, ears, bottom and surrounding area, and the creased areas under the legs and arms.

- Keep the skin between your baby's fingers and toes clean.

- Once your baby's umbilical cord has healed and you're ready to place them in their newborn tub, keep the water shallow (two or three inches deep) while remembering to test the water with your elbow.

- Avoid pouring water directly over your little one's face when washing their hair.

- Trim your little one's nails with a nail file or buffer.

- Avoid touching, picking, and squeezing any skin irritations on your baby.

Diapers and Diaper Rash

Changing a diaper is something you'll do several times a day, but the fortunate thing about this is that you'll quickly get the hang of it after a few practice goes. To make the experience a little quicker, here are key pointers worth keeping in mind.

Preparation

When changing your little one's diaper, the goal is to keep the bottom area clean, moisturized, and dry at all times. To keep you from needing to leave your changing spot to grab more essentials, gather the following supplies before beginning the diaper change:

- a disposable nappy or regular diaper

- a towel or cloth to place under your baby

- wet wipes, damp cotton balls, or a damp washcloth

- petroleum jelly, aqueous cream, or a diaper ointment of your choice

What You Should Know About the Actual Changing Process

To simplify the process of changing your little one's diaper, here are the key points you should always keep in mind:

- Always wipe your baby from the front of their behind to the back.

- Most times, urinary tract infections (UTIs) in girls are caused by wiping their behinds from the back to the front.

- In addition to the baby's buttocks, ensure you also get in between any creased areas around that area.

- Babies urinate all over the place when they're exposed to air.

- Wrap each disposable diaper that's been used in a bag to prevent it from causing your home to smell.

- Avoid flushing used diapers, cotton balls, or baby wipes.

- Avoid overtightening your baby's diaper when you fasten it, and don't make it too loose either because that will cause urine or feces to leak.

- Avoid covering your baby's umbilical cord stump with the diaper's waistline.

- Wash your hands before and after changing your baby's diaper.

- Place a boy's penis in a downward position each time you fasten the diaper.

- With cloth diapers, you can choose between traditional and modern types.

- Oversize pins are always best for cloth diapers that require pinning.

- Avoid mixing used cloth diapers with other laundry.

- Pull-up diapers, disposable underwear, all-in-one diapers, pocket diapers, and fitted diapers are the different types available on the market.

Diaper Rash

Skin irritation, also known as dermatitis, is a common condition among babies, particularly when they wear diapers. Usually, this happens when the baby's bottom and surrounding areas, like the genitals and thighs, are often wet or sensitive, with diapers not being changed frequently enough. Here, the skin will be itchy and tender while appearing to have sores on it. This will often cause your baby to be uncomfortable and irritable (Mayo Clinic, 2022a). Seeing a diaper rash may leave you worried, but, thankfully, the condition is treatable with methods you can try at home. This includes giving your baby's bottom time to air dry, changing your baby's nappy frequently, and using an ointment or baby cream like aqueous cream.

Anytime you notice a diaper rash accompanied by a fever, a rash that doesn't improve after applying home remedies, bleeding, itching, or oozing, then it may be time for you to visit a doctor. Complications like a change in skin color and infections can cause the rash to not heal as it should. If your baby begins to cry when they urinate, it may be a sign that the rash is causing them either pain or a burning sensation each time they urinate or release a stool. A health-care professional can always prescribe medication to help treat the condition or look into other reasons that could be causing the condition to worsen, like a dietary zinc deficiency.

When it comes to what causes a diaper rash, common reasons include

- having your baby's bottom sit too long in a wet or soiled diaper, especially when they have diarrhea

- fastening diapers so tightly that they cause chafing and rubbing

- trying a new product

- feeding your baby a new kind of food

- having an existing skin condition

- taking antibiotics

- having a yeast or bacterial infection (Mayo Clinic, 2018).

From the points mentioned above, we can see that triggering a diaper rash is often due to our everyday decisions as parents—this isn't to apportion blame, but rather to show us that even with changing our baby's diaper regularly, fastening diapers comfortably, and not changing our baby's diet or skin routine, existing skin conditions, medication, and infections can also cause a diaper rash. However, you can avoid the chances of triggering this by

- changing your baby's diaper as often as you can so their bottom area remains clean and dry at all times

- ensuring you rinse your baby's buttocks with lukewarm water each time you change them

- allowing the skin on your baby's bottom to dry first before applying any ointment

- applying a paste, ointment, or diaper cream with every nappy change

- ensuring that you wash your hands after handling a diaper

- fastening your baby's diaper in such a way that it fits comfortably

- allowing your baby's bottom to be free sometimes by having them not wear a diaper for about an hour or so

Clothing and Dressing Considerations

Choosing clothes for your newborn baby can be one of the most exciting things you do in preparation for your little one. But aside from ensuring that your little one has enough clothes and that they're all color coordinated, there are some considerations you should also keep in mind:

- **Safety**: Not all baby clothing is baby friendly; therefore, you must choose clothing items that don't feature hazardous things like buttons, drawstrings, hooks, and bows. Babies can easily choke or strangle themselves with little items that are small enough to put in their mouths. Therefore, it's best to stick to pieces with poppers and zips.

- **Fit**: You want to ensure you purchase your little one clothes that are just the right size so they can offer a snuggly fit. And then when they start moving around a lot more, you can buy them pieces made from flame-resistant fabrics.

- **Fabric**: Pay close attention to the materials being used to make the baby clothes that you buy. Because a baby's skin is sensitive and likely to respond to any irritation, stay clear of pieces made from nylon and polyester. When it comes to fabrics that are usually great for babies' sensitive skin, rayon, cotton, and azlon are always best.

- **Comfort, functionality, and style**: Style, color, and design are the key factors we look for when buying our children's clothes. However, functionality and comfort should be just as important. When we talk about functionality, we simply mean that, knowing we will be changing diapers and feeding our baby every few hours, we may want to invest in clothing items that are easy to slip on and take off. Also, although we'll be taking our babies into public spaces from time to time, we need to remember that these little beings are at home the majority of the time. This means making sure that we get them clothes that are comfortable for sleep and being put down. There's a lot we can get away with when it comes to cutting corners on baby essentials; however, good quality clothing is key. Because babies are changed several times a day, we'll likely have a lot of laundry to do. Good quality clothes are easy to wash and long lasting, despite being washed multiple times. So, to keep our laundry pretty straightforward, we should avoid buying clothes that have special laundry instructions.

- **Season**: Babies grow exceptionally fast, which means they outgrow their clothes just as quickly. Each time a new season is approaching, consider buying baby clothes and shoes that are about one size bigger than your baby is now. This will help you reduce the need to buy new clothes and shoes regularly, since the sizes of the pieces will accommodate your baby's growing needs.

Buying Clothes for a Newborn Baby

It's up to you whether you intend to buy or borrow clothing for your newborn baby, but before they are born, it's always ideal to limit your pieces to a few basics. Apart from possibly spending way too much money buying a lot of things that you'll later no longer need, babies sometimes arrive with skin conditions that may require you to be very particular when it comes to fabric choices. Also, not all babies are born the same size. By buying only the basics, you give yourself a trial-and-error period that won't have you stressed about returns and spending a lot of money on the wrong things.

Cotton happens to be the best clothing fabric for babies, because it's

- soft and gentle on any type of baby skin

- a comfortable clothing choice

- highly breathable

- highly absorbent

- a hypoallergenic fabric

- durable

- easy to clean

- eco-friendly

- biodegradable and natural (Funny Bear, 2023).

Instead of tight-fitting clothing, prioritize buying close-fitting clothes so the item doesn't feel too loose or tight on your baby. Also, check the label on clothing items to check that they're fire resistant. When clothes are flowy and long, they can easily catch fire in the event of an electric shock or heater accident. Of course, newborn babies don't move around a lot, but anything is possible in this day and age, and accidents do happen. With fire-resistant clothes, your baby won't immediately catch fire when there's a flame around.

Before dressing your little one in something for the first time, closely inspect the piece and ensure you've put the item in the laundry first to remove any unwanted bacteria on the clothes. Should you find any unnecessary decorations or loose items that can easily be grabbed or swallowed, remove them immediately so you don't place your child at risk of choking. Check their booties, socks, and mittens too. These clothing items often have loops and threads in them, and, sometimes, babies get their fingers and toes twisted around those threads and loops, which you will want to avoid.

Feeding and Nutrition

Nowadays, we, as mothers, are fortunate to have a variety of feeding options that we can choose from. From breastfeeding and mixed feeding to formula feeding and donor milk, unless there are any medical reasons, what we decide to use will depend entirely on us.

It would be a good idea to speak to a lactation consultant or research the different types of feeding options you have, including the pros and cons of each one. This will help you make a more informed decision and choose the option that will work for you *and* your little one. Many postpartum mothers opt for breastfeeding as their preferred method of feeding. However, issues concerning a low milk supply, conditions like HIV that make it risky to breastfeed babies, and unbearable pain and discomfort, as well as mothers who have either adopted a newborn baby or had a baby through surrogacy, are some of the main reasons many mothers are unable to breastfeed. So, it's important not to establish a community of postpartum mothers who judge mothers who choose to not breastfeed. Remember, it's likely not because they find other feeding options "easier," don't want their breasts to sag, or choose to be selfish.

Breastfeeding Basics

Before birth, most mothers are made to believe that their bodies will naturally be able to produce an abundant supply of breastmilk. That's because while you're pregnant, the glands in your breasts responsible for producing milk start to grow and develop, thanks to hormones like pro-lactin, progesterone, and estrogen. These hormones prepare your breasts for feeding when your little one arrives. So, with time, you'll notice your breasts growing in size. Another change that you may also notice includes a darker areola. All these visible changes are a good sign that your hormones are doing what they should to prepare for the journey to come.

Breastfeeding should begin immediately after birth. This means giving it a go within the first hour of your baby being born. Needing guidance on how to breastfeed a newborn baby isn't something to be ashamed of, as most mothers rely on the help of nursing staff to guide them on how to breastfeed correctly. Over the next few hours and days, you and your baby will spend a lot of time working on latching basics, but while this happens, don't panic if your little one doesn't seem to be "eating enough."

When my little one arrived, the fact they were feeding in short spurts left me pretty concerned because I always imagined my baby consuming cups of breastmilk at a go. But after consulting with a nurse on why my little one seemingly had no appetite, I learned that a newborn baby doesn't need much to get full since their tummies are likely the size of a toy marble (*How Much Milk Your Baby Needs*, n.d.). This means they can take about one to two teaspoons of breastmilk and be full. But, despite their less-than-demanding need to feed, you must make as many attempts as possible to breastfeed, as this is the only way you can encourage your body to produce more milk. By not breastfeeding as often as you should, you risk reducing your milk supply. So, even if your baby isn't feeding as much as you'd expected, the effort you're making to do it often will help your body produce more milk because, with time, your baby's stomach will grow, which means they will eventually be consuming bottles of milk in a day.

If you are recovering from a C-section, you may find it slightly challenging to breastfeed. However, with enough support and guidance on correctly positioning yourself and your newborn baby, you can find a healthy and comfortable way to breastfeed. It's important to speak out about any concerns or questions you may have about breastfeeding. With your baby not being able to openly say, "Mommy, I'm hungry," or "Mommy, I feel I'm unable to latch onto your breast correctly," every bit of training from an experienced mother, midwife, or doula can be of help.

When it comes to latching, it's effective when your baby can suck milk from your breast without needing assistance in the form of you squeezing your breast. When your baby establishes a good breastfeeding latch, this will help increase your milk supply; however, make it a priority to get this right, otherwise you may develop sore nipples and blisters. Many mothers go through a period of trial and error when it comes to getting their baby's latch right, but a good way to tell that they are latching onto your breast properly is by having them take your entire nipple and areola in their mouth. You'll also find their lips turning outward while having their nose and chin make contact with your breast. These are all signs that your little one is latching on to your breast well.

On top of the latching, you need to also work on the positions you and your baby will be most comfortable in while breastfeeding. When you breastfeed for the first time, the process may feel unusual and uncomfortable. Therefore, to achieve a good breastfeeding latch, you need to find a comfortable breastfeeding position that works for you and your baby. There are, of course, different holds that you can ask your midwife or doula to help you with, but don't feel too pressured to take everyone else's word for it. In your quiet time, try finding your own way to breastfeed effectively. The choice is ultimately yours, but when it comes to the best positions you can try if your little one is struggling to latch on to your breast correctly, the cross-cradle and laid-back positions are generally the most helpful. If you notice a few good positions, don't feel the need to stick to one. Alternate between your favorites so different parts of your breasts can be drained of milk effectively.

Breastfeeding can be challenging for many mothers, but you aren't alone. This is a struggle that many mothers face, and, from experience, the best way you can work through it is by seeking support and help. By finding a professional who can investigate any underlying issues or provide you with the solutions and answers you need, you can work through common breastfeeding challenges like

- not producing enough breastmilk

- worrying about whether or not your baby is being fed enough

- not knowing what to do with excess breastmilk

- being unsure of which breastfeeding supplies to have

- wondering why you're so exhausted

- not knowing when exactly to start offering solids

Breastfeeding every few hours can be extremely tiring; however, on top of ensuring that your little one's being fed enough, you also need to feed as often as you can so your body can produce more milk. By the time your baby arrives, your body should have already prepared itself for lactating. To alert your body that it needs to continue producing milk, you need to get your baby on your breast as soon as they arrive. And, to encourage your body to produce more milk as your baby grows, you need to feed as often as you can. When you couple this with proper latching, your body should be producing more than enough milk. To confirm that your little one is getting enough milk, you can check that they're

- gaining steady weight

- soaking six to eight diapers in a day

- experiencing frequent bowel movements

Bottle-Feeding Essentials

Breastfeeding remains the number one feeding option that experts and health-care professionals recommend. It comes with numerous health benefits; however, for mothers who may need or want to explore other alternatives, there's always the formula option. One of the most convenient ways to serve your little one their breastmilk or formula is through a bottle, and it's through bottle-feeding that mothers can enjoy benefits like

- **convenience**: you have the luxury to feed your baby anywhere and at any time

- **flexibility**: you can always pump breastmilk for your little one before heading to work, dropping them off at daycare, or going out to a public space

- **bonding**: you and your partner can use feeding time to bond with your child

- **tracking**: you can monitor how much your baby is drinking

When it comes to bottle-feeding essentials, this can be pretty challenging when you're a first-time mom. So, on your list, it's vital to ensure you have the following:

- at least three feeding bottles

- teats

- a bottle brush

- sterilizing equipment, including a steam sterilizer, a microwave, or a cold-water sterilizer

Choosing a feeding bottle, brush, and sterilizing equipment is relatively straightforward; however, knowing which teat to buy may be a little tricky. Thankfully, there's no evidence that any specific type of teat is better than the next. Instead, the simpler the bottle and teat are, the easier they'll be to clean. One thing you should keep in mind, however, is that you may want to invest in teats that will mimic a natural nursing experience. This means buying teats with a slow-flow nipple as these will allow the milk to flow in a way that feels exactly the same as if your baby were sucking it from your breast. For breastfeeding mothers who are also using bottles to serve their breastmilk, a slow-flow nipple will help prevent nipple confusion (Felton, 2023).

In choosing and preparing any formula bottle, follow these quick and easy steps:

1. Wash your hands thoroughly before handling your baby's bottles and teats.

2. Ensure your feeding bottle essentials are clean and sterilized before using them to feed your baby.

3. Sanitize the area you'll be using to prepare the formula.

4. If you're preparing the infant formula from scratch, ensure you use warm distilled or purified water that's been pre-boiled. Never use water directly from the tap to prepare your baby's formula; there are still risks even if the water is boiled, especially for newborns and immunocompromised babies. Babies should only drink formula prepared with boiled water that has been distilled or purified, so the bacteria and germs found in infant formula can be killed. Always remember, infant formula is not sterile

5. While preparing the formula, be sure to follow the instructions that are shared on the product packaging. Avoid using too much or too little water, as too much water may overly dilute the nutrients in the powdered infant formula, while too little water may dehydrate your baby since the drink will be more concentrated than it should be.

6. If you want to warm up your already-prepared formula or pumped breastmilk, place the bottle in boiling water and check the milk as often as possible to ensure you remove the bottle when the milk is warm rather than hot. In warming the bottle, never take the milk out of the bottle to heat it on the stove, and avoid using a microwave at all costs. Using a microwave can heat the milk unevenly, causing little "hot spots" that will eventually burn your little one's throat and mouth.

7. Before feeding, always check that your baby's milk isn't hot. You can do this by dropping a few drops of the milk on the back of your hand. If it stings, it's too hot. Always ensure the bottle's teat doesn't touch your skin while you do this.

Once your baby's bottle is ready for feeding, make 100% sure that you're following proper bottle-feeding techniques:

- Make sure you and your baby are comfortable during feeds.

- Use this time to bond with each other by holding your baby the right way, making eye contact, and talking to them.

- Always support your baby's head and neck so they can swallow and breathe comfortably.

- Your baby should always be in a semi-upright position during feeds.

- Instead of initiating a feed by forcing the teat into your little one's mouth, gently brush it against their lips and slowly insert it when they open their mouth.

- Afford your baby the time they need to feed, and be careful not to rush them.

- Never leave your baby alone with a bottle in their mouth, as this could choke them without you knowing.

- Always hold your baby's bottle in a horizontal and slightly tipped position.

- Allow your baby to guide you on how the feed is going.

- Wind your baby during short breaks.

- Avoid storing any unused breastmilk or formula.

Sleep and Soothing

When babies are born, they cannot tell the difference between night and day. With no exposure to light and dark in the physical world, their bodies are initially unable to respond to any of the physical, behavioral, and mental changes that occur every 24 hours (National Institute of General Medical Sciences, 2023). At about three to four months of age, their physical environment will start to influence their circadian rhythms and that's how their bodies will become responsive to being awake during the day and going to sleep at night.

As your newborn doesn't yet have a circadian rhythm, you're tasked with supporting any decision your little one's body may make around sleeping during the day and being awake at night. Because your body has already established its circadian rhythm to remain awake during the day and desire rest at night, the times you and your baby set aside to get rest may clash. And because you're in charge of nursing your baby, it becomes your responsibility to adjust your sleep pattern so it works with that of your child. Otherwise, you may gradually become a miserable mother since you won't be getting the hours of sleep you need.

Unlike dealing with a toddler, young child, or teenager, sending your newborn baby to bed isn't as simple as issuing a "go to bed" instruction. You're simply tasked with sleeping when your baby sleeps and keeping your baby company when they're awake. This will, unfortunately, be your new way of life until your baby's circadian rhythm is finally established. There isn't any "treatment" plan you can use to activate your baby's circadian rhythm; however, you can speed up the process of adjusting their rhythm by exposing your little one to natural light during the day. You can also create a dark bedroom setting for your baby at night. This will help train your baby to know when it's day and night. Thankfully, you're designed to release hormones that signal your body to stay awake during the day and feel tired and in need of rest at night.

It's crucial to ensure that you help your baby get the hours of sleep they need. Over time, this affects their cognition, physical growth, overall development, and body functions like executive function, language, and memory. Affording your child the sleep they need will work in their favor in the long run, since it will improve how their memory and brain process information.

Now that we understand the importance of having your little one get enough sleep, and why they follow a sleep rhythm that's different from an adult's or older child's, it's time to answer the big question: "How much sleep does my baby need?" From birth to about three months of age, your little one should be getting between 14 and 17 hours of sleep each day. From 4 to 11 months, these hours will lessen to about 12 to 15 hours of sleep each day. And then, once they're one to two years of age, they'll need about 11 to 14 hours of sleep in a day.

Occasionally, you may be tempted to consider keeping your little one awake during the day so they're exhausted and easier to put to bed by nighttime. It's an idea that most mothers silently consider when they're trying to get a good night's sleep; however, you shouldn't try to adjust an infant's sleep schedule. A baby's circadian rhythm should form naturally, as adjusting it yourself may affect the hours your child will get to rest. This could easily develop into a sleep problem that will ultimately affect their behavior and learning in the long run. So, just for the time being, consider taking naps with your little one as often as you can. And when it comes to the household chores and any other commitments you may have, consider cutting yourself some slack by either asking for assistance or not being too hard on yourself when the dishes aren't done or the sitting room's a little messy. When you and your little one are finally awake, strap them on in a baby carrier or wrap and do as much cleaning as possible. Remember, it's not for ever.

Baby Cues and Communication

Because you and your baby are working on establishing a relationship with one another, you need to develop a language that you'll both understand. Your patterns and habits will communicate what you need your baby to know, but it's equally important to train yourself on how your baby communicates with you. Baby cues are your baby's language of communication, and it's important that you learn these to help you

- build healthy habits with your baby from an early stage

- train your child to do things like sleep and feed

- notice any odd behavior

- foster their brain development

- respond to their needs to assure them that you've acknowledged their emotions

- establish a sense of trust between you and your baby

Babies often have common baby cues and body language that you can use to recognize and interpret the message they're trying to get across. Common body language signs include

- **Arching back**: This could mean they're experiencing a sense of discomfort in their stomach, especially during feeds. It could indicate gastrointestinal reflux, satiety, colic, or heartburn. They arch their backs to try and relieve them from the discomfort; therefore, the best way to comfort them would be to rub their back for a while.

- **Ear-grabbing**: Babies grab their ears when they've just discovered them or are teething. If the ear-grabbing is accompanied by a cold or fever, it could indicate that they have an ear infection. Teething toys can help ease their discomfort, but you should consult a doctor if their ear-grabbing comes with other signs like a sleeping problem or stuffy nose.

- **Head-banging**: Head-banging is the rhythmic movement a baby makes by rocking their head back and forth. Babies use this as a self-soothing technique right before taking a nap or heading for bedtime. Most babies will typically stop the habit as they grow older, but you must keep an eye on them when they are still engaging in this behavior as they may hit their head on a hard surface. To do this, you can pad their cradle walls to prevent any injuries from happening. Because they're still young and unable to understand when you try to share your concerns, finding ways to stop the habit may prove to be fruitless.

- **Constant kicking**: Newborn babies will kick a lot when they're happy and excited. Don't be too alarmed when you find them stretching their legs the way they do, as this is their way of exercising their leg muscles in preparation for their rolling period. Depending on what other body language your baby displays, constant kicking could also mean they're uncomfortable. You can tell this if they have a grumpy look on their face. In expressing their discomfort, they may be trying to tell you that they're either bloated or in need of a diaper change. If they appear to be bloated, try relieving them by burping them. You can also consider your diet by checking what foods you are eating that could be triggering gas that you may be passing to your baby during breastfeeding.

- **Grumpiness**: Babies can look unsettled or grumpy when they're in unfamiliar spaces or doing an unusual activity. Anything out of their everyday routine could leave them feeling overwhelmed and overstimulated. Therefore, this could be their sign to you that they need some quiet time. It may not be practical at the time to simply get up and leave, so consider taking them to a quiet spot and rocking them until they calm down. Playing their favorite song or taking them out for some fresh air may also do the trick. This may take a while, but the last thing you want to do is return them to the same setting without calming them first, so afford them the time they need to settle down a bit.

- **Fist-clenching**: Babies clench their fists as a primitive reflex that their bodies do naturally, and it usually stops after about five to six months of age. If you see your baby doing this shortly after birth, there's no need to worry about it because they're simply continuing the habit, which started when they were still inside the womb. It's a natural habit that most babies have, but be careful of this habit as it may also indicate that your little one is stressed or hungry.

- **Hiccups**: Babies experience many occurrences of hiccups until about one year old. Because they happen when your baby is fed too quickly or overfed, they're nothing to worry about since hiccups usually go away within 5 to 10 minutes. If you notice that your little one experiences hiccups after every feed, adjust the position you're using to feed the baby and ensure you burp them after each feed. Another reason your baby may be experiencing hiccups often is because they may not be latching onto your breast the right way. So, you may want to double-check your technique there as well.

- **Arm jerks**: An arm jerk could be a sign that your little one's been disturbed by a bright light that's caught their attention while sleeping or a loud sound. It's an involuntary movement that they usually outgrow, but you may want to keep your little one from loud noises and lights if they interfere with their sleep, as this could exhaust them over time. If your baby happens to wake up due to a loud sound, respond to their cue by comforting them and putting them back in their sleep spot. You can either quiet the space or place them in a more comfortable sleep environment that will allow them to get the rest they need.

- **Eye-rubbing**: Babies will rub their eyes when they're tired, which is their sign to you that they're ready for a nap or to go to sleep. This will usually be accompanied by droopy eyelids and a bit of yawning from time to time; however, if the eye-rubbing is causing their eyes to turn red, this could mean they're experiencing some kind of irritation in the eye. Pollen is a common cause of eye-rubbing among babies. If you do conclude that your little one has a foreign body stuck in their eye, use a sterilized gauze to clean the area around the eye, but avoid making any attempt to touch the eyeball or surrounding area at all costs. In a situation like this, it's best to speak to a pediatrician in case your little one has an infection.

- **Quick breathing**: Quick breathing in a baby could mean two things—they're either startled or struggling to contain their excitement. You'll just have to monitor their body language and facial expressions when they do this. If they're maintaining a happy face while breathing fast, they're just excited at what may be happening at that time. After some minutes, their breathing pattern should return to normal. But if they appear surprised, this could be a reason for them to be breathing faster. When this happens, you should calm them by speaking to them in a soft and reassuring way. You can also try doing something that will take their attention away from what just distracted them.

- **Scrunched knees**: When a baby scrunches their knees, this is usually a sign of feeling bloated and constipated. This happens quite often among newborns, so to ease their discomfort, they will bring their knees to their abdominal area. To be of assistance, gently massage their stomach area in a clockwise direction and ensure you burp them well after every feed. Again, if you're breastfeeding, take a moment to look into your diet because there could be something you're eating that's causing your little one to become extremely bloated.

- **Turning their face the other way**: You may take your baby turning their face away from you as a sign of rejection. However, a baby may do this when they're bored or trying to tell you they're full and no longer need to be fed. If you're in an unfamiliar setting or surrounded by moving objects or visuals, your little one could be moving their head around to see what's happening around them. It's a milestone worth celebrating because it shows that your baby is growing and developing as they should. If you need more ideas on how to keep your baby entertained, start a new activity or take them out on a walk. And if they're telling you they're feeling full and overfed, stop the feeding immediately and don't try to force-feed them.

- **Sucking fingers**: Babies use a sucking reflect to latch onto a bottle or breast; therefore, when you find them sucking their finger, this could be a sign they're hungry. So, when you see them doing this, try feeding them immediately. Some babies will use their finger-sucking habit as a way to soothe themselves, and you'll pick up on that when you see them continue to suck their fingers even after being fed. If you feel a little uncomfortable about them sucking their fingers as a self-soothing technique, instead of stopping the habit completely, try using a pacifier.

- **Bearing down, grunting, and grimacing**: Babies often express their great discomfort by grimacing, bearing down, or grunting before and during pooping. Their actions may intensify if they're constipated, but to help with the process, you could rub their belly gently. You may be concerned if their release is accompanied by a bit of crying, but check their poop for any abnormalities in their stool. Sometimes, hard stools may be difficult for them to release, so if this is the case, try getting your little one in an exercise routine. Doing something as simple as encouraging them to cycle their legs could help stimulate movements in their intestines. And to help prevent any further constipation, if you are breastfeeding you may want to consider checking your own diet.

Understanding Different Cries and Their Meanings

Babies cry a lot; therefore, it's a good idea to have some understanding of what they may be trying to tell you. So, here's a quick summary of your baby's different cries and what they mean:

- "Neh": Your little one is hungry.

- "Eh": Your baby is signaling that they have some upper wind they'd like to release with a burp.

- "Eairh": Your baby is flooded with lower wind and would like to pass some gas.

- "Heh": They're trying to express their discomfort by letting you know they're either hot, wet, or cold.

- "Owh": They're sleepy and ready for bed.

Safety and First Aid

Here are quick points to remember regarding safety and first aid when you have a newborn baby.

Creating a Safe Environment for Your Baby

Always ensure your baby's physical surroundings are safe by

- arranging your household items and furniture to make it easy for you to see your baby at all times

- keeping the spaces you use for tummy time away from areas where other children may be playing or adults may be walking

- surrounding your baby with age-appropriate items only

- keeping hot foods, liquids, and surfaces out of reach

- ensuring your furniture is bolted and secured at all times.

- keeping wires and extension cords far from reach.

- checking your baby's surroundings don't have any small objects lying around as they may put them in their mouth and swallow them

- using safety devices like carbon monoxide detectors and smoke alarms all around the house

- keeping toys, furniture, cribs, and any objects your baby may be handling away from windows

- keeping your pets away from the baby

- keeping the baby's surroundings clear of any clutter

Traveling Safely

When traveling with your newborn baby, always place them in a car seat suitable for their weight, age, and height. Install the car seat correctly at all times and double-check it to ensure your little one is strapped in safely and securely. When your baby is still a newborn, they need to remain in the back seat of the vehicle. Under no circumstances should you ever leave your baby unattended in the car, as accidents can happen at any moment.

Common Household Hazards and How to Avoid Them

Common household hazards you should always manage include

- keeping household detergents and glass items out of reach and locked away

- keeping poisonous items, including indoor and outdoor plants, out of reach

- storing medication out of reach at all times

- avoiding the use of chemicals or strongly scented products around your newborn baby

Basic First Aid for Common Baby Injuries

To treat minor baby injuries, you should always have the following first aid items on hand:

- an antibiotic ointment

- an adhesive bandage

While cleaning a wound and removing any debris, be sure to use plain water. Should the injury need a lot more than the items listed above, then it is a good idea to visit the hospital immediately, especially if the injury is related to a burn, a broken bone, or a major cut.

Next Steps

Your mental and emotional self-care is just as important as physical care for you and your baby. In the next chapter, we'll explore how to prioritize yourself just as much as you prioritize your baby's needs, because you're both worth it and deserve all the care there is for bringing life into this world.

Chapter Three

YOU'RE NOT LOSING YOUR MIND

No one talks about the low moments—the pressure you feel, the incredible letdown every time you hear the baby cry. I've broken down, I don't know how many times. Or I'll get angry about the crying, then sad about being angry, and then guilty, like, 'Why do I feel so sad when I have a beautiful baby?

Serena Williams

The birth of a child is a life-changing experience for many mothers. But while you work on embracing motherhood and establishing a relationship with your newborn baby, your mind and emotions are at play. From anxiety and fear to joy and disbelief, it's an intense roller coaster of mixed ideas and feelings clouding your mind. Because this is your first time going through all these experiences all at once, it may be hard to make sense of the mood swings, sleep difficulties, panic attacks, and crying spells; however, if your baby blues are carrying on for longer than two weeks postpartum, this could be a sign of postpartum depression.

Also known as peripartum depression, this severe and long-lasting kind of depression can begin during the gestation period and after the birth of your baby (Mayo Clinic, 2022b). Thankfully, a lot of awareness is spreading about conditions like postpartum depression and postpartum psychosis, which is a more extreme mood disorder that can also develop after birth. We still have a long way to go in changing the narrative that postpartum depression is a weakness or flaw. But with the proper support and immediate treatment, you can receive the help you need to manage your symptoms and work through any difficulties you may be having.

It's extremely important to monitor your mental health during your postpartum journey. Although you may find yourself physically able to wake up in the mornings, take care of your baby, run your home, and cover your personal basics like bathing daily and eating the right diet, the condition of your mind will start affecting how you feel about motherhood as a whole. Feeling confused, lost, and beside yourself, you may begin to dread motherhood since parenting is highly demanding. And with the other personal challenges you may be going through, you may find yourself overwhelmed the majority of the time. So, the moment your little one cries a little longer than they normally do, is restless, or wakes up from a nap that you just put them down for, this may leave you stressed, on edge, unhappy, and feeling all kinds of negative emotions.

If you're already going through the baby blues and wondering what in the world is going on with you, don't worry—you're not alone, and you aren't losing your mind. You simply need some self-care and a bit of physical, emotional, and mental support. So, before you allow someone else to make you feel like you're playing weak or looking for attention, here's a chapter dedicated to understanding where you are mentally and how you can overcome your challenges.

It's More Common Than You Think

Nowadays, many mothers are coming forth to share their stories on the realities that come with motherhood right after birth. In reading story after story, I've come to learn that we all go through common experiences like the following:

- It's pretty normal for mothers to keep their concerns and frustrations to themselves because they fear not being heard or taken seriously by their partners, those closest to them, or health-care professionals.

- Even health-care professionals remain ignorant of issues concerning maternal mental health.

- People often brush us off with comments like, "I don't understand what's wrong with you" and "Don't worry—it's just the baby blues. It'll wear off soon enough."

- Our support systems typically focus on physical healing and how to nurse a newborn baby.

- Most women feel alone during the bittersweet journey of motherhood.

- People often believe a bit of makeup, a shopping spree, or a quick cleanup is all we need to overcome any baby blues we may have.

- Doctors prefer waiting until we have a complete meltdown and are admitted to a psychiatric ward before offering us any assistance or a prescription.

- People, including health-care providers, usually judge mothers who are suffering from postpartum depression and anxiety.

- We're often misdiagnosed because health-care providers don't ask the right questions.

- Many mothers are faced with having to deal with unsupportive spouses and toxic relationships.

- The lack of access to resources to help mothers navigate through their journeys right after birth leaves us feeling lost, confused, and alone.

- Trauma during birth adds to the fears and anxieties mothers go through.

- We sometimes mistake depression for just normal anxiety or pressure from being new moms when in fact, we're living through depression without consciously realizing it.

Strange dreams, intrusive thoughts, self-doubt, millions of questions, mom guilt, paranoia, and loneliness are some of the many thoughts in our minds. But instead of suffering on the inside, doing everything to brush the negativity off or block it, or telling ourselves, *My body will alert me when there's something wrong*, we should take a moment to realize that we're not alone. Millions of mothers go through the same concerns, doubts, and experiences, but we shouldn't leave it to health-care professionals, those we hold dear to our hearts, or our negative thought patterns to do all the concluding. With a bit of knowledge and a few tips and tricks, we can work on any mental health issues we may have, even if it means attempting it all on our own first.

Our Physical State Affects Our Mental Health

Different variables contribute to your mental health; however, one of the most significant contributors is the state of our physical well-being. When you go the extra mile to ensure you nurture and take care of yourself physically, you automatically prioritize your personal needs and follow a lifestyle that supports your mental health. And by looking good, you then feel good about yourself, which helps you cope with any stress and depression you may be going through.

When our mental health is in poor condition, we begin to entertain negative thought patterns that ultimately cripple us into believing we're worthless and undeserving of good things. When we leave these negative thoughts to live in us rent-free, we experience a significant change in how we think, feel, and treat ourselves as a whole. So, by nurturing and taking care of ourselves, we can reduce the chances of suffering from the symptoms and conditions of mental illness.

Of course, motherhood will likely mean you are far from having all the time in the world to indulge in self-care; however, you don't always need an expensive gift or five-star restaurant experience to feel good about yourself. With small efforts like exercising regularly, eating healthily, meditating, doing self-affirmations, and getting some fresh air from time to time, you can make meaningful improvements to your physical health. In questioning what you can do to improve your physical health, ask yourself, *Will this make me happier and more content?* If so, then do it. Realizing that exercise, healthy eating, meditation, self-affirmations, and getting out a bit are necessities and not luxuries will help keep you consistent and committed to improving your physical well-being.

In Chapter 1, we talked about the importance of self-care and the components every postpartum mother should prioritize in healing her physical body. Of course, we covered different things you should do, but in getting you to have a healthy mindset, the following physical health habits should be exercised as often as possible:

- **Nutrition**: Especially if you're a breastfeeding mother, you need to ensure you get the right amount of nutrition. But in shifting the attention to you for a second, your postpartum body needs all the nutrients it can get to remain resourceful and active. To attain good physical health, eating foods with several vitamins and minerals can do a lot of good. Plus, prioritizing carbohydrates and proteins can provide the perfect balance.

- **Activity**: People often believe postpartum mothers lose their shape and don't exercise much because they're "lazy" or "don't feel like it"; however, this is far from true. Yes, newborn babies take naps, and, as an outsider looking in, this would be the perfect time to get a quick gym or exercise session in. But between complete exhaustion, physical healing, and other household responsibilities, sometimes all you want to do in your spare time is sleep or just laze around. This will truly be the first time you'll understand what it means when they say, "Choosing to do nothing is also a plan." I know it's hard, but prioritizing physical activity isn't just for the moms who want a "banging body" and "snatched waist." It's also for your health, because physical activity and other self-care essentials all work together to provide you with good overall health.

According to research, your postpartum journey begins right after birth (Lopez-Gonzalez & Kopparapu, 2022). This is the time your body will adjust its hormone levels, uterus size, and physique to a state of no longer being pregnant. So, it's safe to say that this is a period you eventually get through, but the huge adaptions usually take about one year to work through for your mental, emotional, and physical wellbeing.

It's a critical period for any mother and child, but when there's a lack of support and help, both the mother and child could end up going through a complete phase of sheer neglect. On top of going through labor and the physical birth of a child, you still have procedures and physical wounds that you need to heal from. Unfortunately, a child's need for food, care, and warmth doesn't pause while they wait for you to get through what you need to get through. You're faced with the task of being a mother while taking care of yourself in the best way possible, and you're expected to thrive at this all while maintaining personal routines, coping with mood disturbances, and not getting enough sleep.

Self-Awareness and Mindfulness

While validation is important in helping mothers manage their postpartum journey, taking active steps to control your thoughts and feelings is equally important. By understanding how your thought patterns influence your emotions, it becomes easier to work toward attaining a healthy and positive mindset. This is possible when you focus your attention on self-awareness and mindfulness.

Understanding Thoughts and Feelings

Our physical health is a lot easier to work through because we can lose all the baby weight, watch our blood pressure drop to a normal rate, or have our skin improve because we're eating more healthily. These are the results we can see. However, our mental state is challenging to imagine, manage, or overcome because we can't physically see it, and we sometimes think we've moved on from something when we haven't, or are no longer bothered by something when we are.

So, what are our thoughts? Our thoughts are the voices that go on inside our heads. Sometimes, we're aware of what the voices in our heads are saying, but sometimes we aren't; therefore, there will be times when we'll think of positive things and there'll be times when we'll think of negative things. In our minds, we have the subconscious mind, which appears when we're unconscious of our physical surroundings. So, when we're asleep or under hypnosis, this is us entering our subconscious mind. We usually have no control over our subconscious mind because it's fed by what goes on in our conscious mind. On the other hand, we have the conscious mind, which plays out when we're conscious of our physical surroundings. This explains why we're able to be aware of our thoughts, so, with knowledge of what we're thinking and saying to ourselves, we can control this part of our minds.

According to research, humans have about 70,000 thoughts in a single day, and 95% of those thoughts are repetitive (*Stuck on Negative Thinking*, n.d.). Of course, this means that if you're more of a positive thinker, you're likely forming positive thought patterns that play out in your mind 95% of the time. However, the same will also be true for negative thinkers: If you're a negative thinker, you're likely forming negative thought patterns that will play out 95% of the time.

Our thoughts fuel our emotions, which means that to feel a certain way, a negative or positive thought would have first fueled that thought. Our actions and reactions will then be sparked by our feelings or minds. Part of growing up means learning to control our emotions, whether those emotions are good or bad. In managing our feelings, we're able to allow our minds to initiate the response and, usually, this will be well thought out and less emotional. So, depending on where you are with your mental state and emotions, your habits will pick one or the other option. Having a basic understanding of how your thoughts and feelings work means you can use this knowledge to guide you on your postpartum journey, as this will improve your overall wellbeing over time.

How Your Postpartum Journey Affects Your Thoughts and Emotions

When you like what you see physically, this feeds positive thoughts in your mind. Therefore, each time you treat yourself, keep your physical surroundings clean, or have an effective routine with your newborn baby, your thoughts are centered around believing you've got the hang of things and are managing your new journey. With more and more positive thoughts, over time, this becomes the 95% of what you're hearing in your head; this will ultimately lead you to positive feelings that will make you feel encouraged, happy, and more hopeful about your journey.

Negative postpartum experiences are often referred to as "baby blues." Most people mistake baby blues for depression; however, depression is a more serious mental illness that you feel trapped in and cannot escape. Baby blues, on the other hand, are feelings of sadness. They usually arrive a few days after giving birth to your baby. About 80% of new mothers go through this phase of their postpartum journey regardless of their age, education, culture, race, or culture (*Baby Blues After Pregnancy*, n.d.).

Although baby blues make you feel like you're not doing something right, these are just thoughts that make you blame yourself for doing something you didn't do. That's because baby blues aren't caused by anything you did wrong. Instead, they're caused by hormonal changes that are taking place in your body, when your estrogen and progesterone levels are low enough to result in frequent mood swings. Sometimes, a woman's thyroid gland also has a part to play, since levels of the hormones it releases may drop significantly. This makes you feel exhausted the majority of the time, and, over time, it could develop into depression.

When we have the baby blues, hormonal changes, and other unpleasant physical experiences, this generates a lot of negativity within us, which is perfectly normal and understandable. And the fact that you may not like the new stretch marks, saggy breasts, hyperpigmentation, baby fat, hair loss, and other postpartum symptoms makes it worse. Plus, if you aren't getting enough support from your partner, close friends, or family, all while facing possible financial struggles, the reality of returning to work once your maternity break is over and having the overwhelming pressure of being a new mom can be a lot to take in and manage.

Of course, you're human, and it's natural to have some kind of negative response to situations that leave you unhappy. We cannot simply switch off when we're dissatisfied with something and then switch back on after. We process every little and significant experience we go through. So, each time our physical surroundings and being aren't satisfying, this feeds negative thoughts in our minds. When this goes on long enough, our thoughts become more and more negative, leading to 95% of the thoughts we hear in our heads also being negative. This amplifies our negative emotions, making us feel overwhelmed, unhappy, and less hopeful about our journey. Thoughts lead to words, which lead to actions, which lead to habits, which ultimately become who we are.

Common Intrusive Thoughts That Most Postpartum Mothers Have

You become the product of your thoughts. This simply means that when you perhaps forget to change your baby's diaper and entertain even the tiniest negative idea, like, *I'm a terrible mother*, this idea can grow from the size of a seed to a fruit in just a matter of seconds. Yes, you may not be happy, overjoyed, and pleased with various circumstances, people, environments, or situations, but be careful of what you feed your mind. You become your thoughts. This means that when you start thinking you're a terrible mother or aren't attractive, you eventually become those things, even if it means becoming that on purpose. Since we aren't always aware of what we're telling ourselves, here are common intrusive thoughts that you may be having from time to time:

- *What if something bad happens to my baby?*

- *What if I'm incapable of loving my baby the way they need to be loved?*

- *What if my baby doesn't connect with me or love me?*

- *What if I'm a burden to my family and those around me?*

- *There are many other mothers who journey through motherhood far better than I can.*

- *I'm no longer as attractive as I used to be.*

- *No man wants this.*

- *My partner probably no longer finds me sexually attractive.*

- *I don't know what I'm doing.*

- *My child deserves a better mother.*

Don't Be Too Quick to Rely on Your Thoughts

When you're down and feel like you've hit rock bottom, it's easy to find yourself getting wrapped up in the different thoughts that may be going on in your mind at the time. And when your thoughts somehow align with your reality, you start believing you are those ideas. But it's important to remember that you aren't your thoughts. Any negative thoughts you may be having at the moment only exist because of your circumstances, your mood, and the relationships you have with yourself and others. When your postpartum journey finally ends, and you're starting to get the hang of things more consistently, these feelings and thoughts will disappear, but who you are as an individual will remain. So, it's important to focus on acknowledging your strengths and rewarding your milestones to affirm yourself so you don't get lost in your thoughts.

Using Self-Awareness and Mindfulness to Reshape Negative Thoughts

Self-awareness is when you become intentional about knowing who you are in terms of your character, desires, feelings, and motives. So, it's when you take the time to focus on yourself, and how every part of your mind and behavior aligns with who you want to be. When you're conscious of this, anytime you're exposed to activities or environments that uplift, motivate, and inspire you, you immediately gravitate toward them because they align with who you're working to become.

Any activities or environments that derail, discourage, and affect you negatively will alert and you'll immediately work on ways to get away from the situation. So, when you're self-aware, you can view yourself objectively and not allow your emotions to get the better of you, because you have a clear way of processing all your thoughts, feelings, and actions without trying too hard to defend yourself each time. Self-awareness is a skill that many of us wish to have; however, it takes a while to perfect because many of us are greatly driven by emotions. But if we practice self-awareness or are on a journey to learn more about ourselves and refine our internal standards, this will allow us to monitor our growth and change any parts of ourselves that we know need improving.

Mindfulness is another skill you can learn to help overcome your negative thought patterns. With mindfulness, you're intentionally allowing yourself to be present in each moment of your life. Sometimes, as mothers, we're often caught up in what used to be, regrets, and weaknesses. Suppose we're not stuck in the past; in that case, we're obsessing over the future—either fearing what's to come, or growing impatient because we can't wait to get back to work, looking forward to our baby getting a little older so they will stop crying all the time, or finally have the body we've been imagining this entire time. We use our past and future as a coping mechanism to not be aware of what we're feeling or experiencing right so this steals us away from enjoying motherhood, even if it means enduring a long postpartum journey.

When you're mindful, you remain aware of each moment on purpose. You're fully engaged in everything happening both within and around and, as you discover more about yourself, you accept every part of yourself and do so without any judgment.

Practicing Mindfulness for Emotional Wellbeing

The negativity bias teaches us that when people don't have a solid mental state, they're more inclined to entertain negative thoughts than positive thoughts at any given moment (Nikolopoulou, 2023). This means that even when we're presented with 100 positive comments in a day, we're more inclined to fix our minds on the one negative comment someone made, making it easier to entertain unhelpful or negative thoughts than positive ones. But regardless of this reality, you have the power to transform your negative thought patterns into positive ones when you exercise any of these habits consistently:

- **The two-column exercise**: This is a great technique that requires you to take a piece of paper and separate it into two columns. On one side, you'll list all your negative thoughts, while listing all your positive ones on the other. The point is not to overthink, defend, or hide anything. You're simply writing down any unhelpful ideas you have going on in your mind at the time. Each time you do this, seeing your inner critic makes you aware of what's clouding your and, with the help of self-awareness, you can immediately work on ways to disassociate yourself from those negative thoughts because they aren't aligning with who you intend to become.

- **Find new evidence**: To a certain extent, your unhealthy thoughts are fueled by some kind of evidence that you're seeing in your physical environment. So, you may feel unattractive because you're not showering as often as you should, usually have your hair in a mess, and are always dressed in baggy, torn clothes. No, you aren't your thoughts, but to reshape these negative thoughts using the truth, you need to present each negative idea with new evidence that will prove that thought untrue.

- **Exercise self-compassion**: With negative thoughts, we often speak to ourselves in a manner, tone, or way that we'd never use on someone else. To become self-aware and more mindful, you have to develop a healthy relationship with yourself, but this won't be possible if you're constantly talking down to yourself every chance you get.

- **Spot the call to action**: Negative thoughts usually inspire us to do something about them, and one of the best ways you can reshape your thought patterns is by journaling your postpartum experience so you can mark every milestone you meet along the way. Yes, we sometimes long for those big wins to feel good about ourselves, but because this will require a bit of time and energy, you'll find your baby steps to be just as meaningful as your large ones.

- **Soften the blow**: Like self-compassion, remember to be kind to yourself. You're human and walking a journey that you've never walked before. Whenever you notice a weakness or mistake, avoid beating yourself up about it. Instead, look at ways you can work on improving your choices. So, stick up for yourself and try being intentional and conscious about it, because this does help in making you feel good a lot of the time.

- **Practice self-acceptance**: Your cycle of negative thoughts can sometimes be vicious, because, on top of already feeling bad about everything negative your mind is telling you, you're also feeling bad about how all these things are being said. This creates a lot of internal resistance because it often causes a lot of internal suffering that's challenging to work through. But instead of trying so hard to block the thoughts out or work even harder to attain "perfection," surrender and don't fight back. When a negative thought arises, pause for a moment and take a minute to notice it. Then tell yourself, *I can love this about myself*. Of course, there are certain things that we should change when the time calls for it. For instance, if your lack of discipline or time management is affecting your role as a mother, it may be a good idea to work on that instead of choosing not to change it in the name of self-acceptance. But when it comes to mistakes or things you can't necessarily change, like your stretch marks, weight gain, or moments of feeling like you're on a roller coaster of emotions, look at each one of these and tell yourself, *You know what—I love that*. Physically telling yourself you love the good and "the bad" about everything that concerns you is a radical exercise in self-acceptance, and it often lightens the mood a bit when you admit, *It's not that bad*. Over time, the tone and manner you use on yourself will improve, gradually reshaping your negative thought patterns.

Top Tips to Stay Mentally Strong After Having Your Baby

Self-care is also about investing in your mental state. But as well as being aware of exercises like meditation, you can do a lot more to improve your mental health right after having a baby. So, here are different ways you can work on taking care of your mental health.

SNOWBALL—Mental Health Techniques to Keep You in Positive Spaces

Mental strength requires you to do a little more than just focus your attention on a single activity. Sure, journaling and meditation can work, but there are other things you can do to make your efforts more effective. SNOWBALL techniques are effective options you can use to improve your mental health (Hill, 2023). Plus, they're practical, which means any postpartum mom can attempt them, regardless of their busy schedule:

- **Sleep**: Make sure you're getting enough sleep—and not just any sleep, but quality sleep. When you're tired on top of having the baby blues, you won't be able to make rational decisions, which could worsen your mood swings within a short amount of time.

- **Nutrition**: We often assume eating healthily is only great for our physical health, but we should also be aware of what it can do for our mind. Maintaining a healthy diet helps your body recover the way it should. So, when you're back being more mobile again and able to get more things done, this gets you in better spirits.

- **Omega-3 fatty acids**: Commit to including fish oils in your diet. They contain omega-3 fatty acids, which help postpartum mothers reduce their levels of depression and anxiety.

- **Walking**: Exercise, even in the form of walking, can improve your mood. Not only does it help you get the fresh air you need to think a little more clearly and calm any negative emotions you may have, it also helps your physical body recover from delivery.

- **Baby breaks**: Having your baby out of sight may be a little overwhelming and scary at first, because you'll likely imagine all sorts of things happening to them while you're away. But to make your break a lot more relaxing, ensure your baby is in the hands of someone you know and trust, like an experienced nanny, close relative, or friend who also has children of their own. This way, you'll know that if anything happens, they'll know what to do. While away, take the time you need to do some much-needed TLC, like getting some sleep or indulging in any form of self-care. This will help you feel good and rejuvenated by the time you return to your little one.

- **Adult time**: With everything you have going on with your newborn baby and personal journey, it may be hard to keep yourself emotionally available for others. But do so. You need this. Spend a bit of time nurturing some of your close relationships and ensure you're present and enjoying the time you're spending with those people.

- **Liquids**: Remember to stay as hydrated as possible. Drink lots of water and try to avoid any physical activities or foods that could leave you feeling dehydrated. This includes spending too much time in the sun or eating foods containing too much salt.

- **Laughter**: Remember to smile and laugh as much as you can. Yes, you're in the postpartum phase of your life, but you're also part of a parenting journey. If you aren't much of a joker, try watching comedy movies or stand-up shows now and then. This will add a lot of humor to your day. Anything to keep you smiling!

Apart from doing the above, always remember the following:

- Be mindful of the company you keep, because this will influence how you feel and think as a whole.

- Get as much sleep as you can.

- Avoid turning down parenting suggestions from professionals or other experienced moms; do what works for you.

- Exercise self-compassion and self-kindness at all times.

- Read and make yourself knowledgeable about the different resources you can use to help you through your postpartum journey.

Seeking Professional Help

The baby blues usually wear off by about two weeks after giving birth. But if your mood swings are accompanied by exhaustion, sadness, and worry, this may be a sign of depression. Postpartum depression (PPD) is a mental illness that many women suffer from after having a baby. According to research, one in every seven women is diagnosed with PPD, which accounts for about 15% of mothers worldwide (*Postpartum Depression*, n.d.). So, while you're sitting and thinking there may be something wrong with you, just know that PPD is a common complication that many women go through after having a baby.

When it comes to the causes, experts and medical professionals aren't exactly sure of what causes PPD; however, links have been spotted with the following factors:

- **Genetics**: If you have a family history of relatives who have previously suffered from depression, the condition will likely pass to you and your children as well, thanks to body cells that collect and store information on how our bodies should operate and grow.

- **Hormonal changes after delivery**: Some of the hormones in our bodies are responsible for controlling the state of our moods and emotions. When we're pregnant, our normal hormonal levels increase to help our bodies do what they need to do while carrying and nurturing our babies for the entire gestation period. Within the first 24 hours of delivery, our hormone levels drop drastically to return to normal and this rapid change is what usually leads many mothers to PPD.

- **Low thyroid hormones**: Our thyroid is a gland located in our neck. It helps us use and store any energy we gather from the food we eat. When we aren't receiving the energy we need to function, this leads many to PPD.

When it comes to the symptoms, the first thing you'll notice is that your "baby blues" phase will last a little longer than the typical two weeks. But sometimes, you can skip the baby blues and head straight into depression just a week after delivery. When this medical condition arrives, it's usually accompanied by daily emotional and mental health symptoms like

- feeling depressed, ashamed, or guilty most of the time

- feeling like you don't know what you're doing and are a failure

- having panic attacks and constant feelings of fear

- suffering from severe mood swings

- no longer taking an interest in the things you used to enjoy doing

- feeling exhausted throughout the day

- experiencing a change in appetite that causes you to eat more or less than you usually would

- experiencing changes in your weight

- struggling to sleep

- not being able to concentrate or make sober-minded decisions

- struggling to establish a bond between you and your baby

- entertaining unhealthy thoughts of harming yourself or your baby

- having thoughts about killing yourself

PPD can affect every aspect of your life, and it's pretty common to find many mothers not taking the condition seriously because they believe it will wear off eventually. While it's normal to brush some things off just so you don't cause any unnecessary panic, PPD does come with the risk of it affecting how you choose to take care of yourself and your baby. This is because when it's left untreated, the following could happen:

- You may no longer be interested in following up with your post-partum appointments.

- You may find it difficult to establish a bond with your newborn baby.

- Because PPD can make it challenging for you and your little one to adapt to breastfeeding, you may need to move to other feeding alternatives.

- When you're depressed, your mind isn't completely focused on your baby and their needs. This will make it difficult for you to spot any medical concerns quickly. Not attending to your baby's medical needs on time could worsen any sicknesses or emergencies they may have. Also, you may not be consistent in keeping up with your baby's appointments, especially when it comes to vaccinations.

- Your little one may suffer from mental health issues and problems concerning their development, behavior, and learning as they grow older.

It's Time to Get Help

When you're having a hard time falling or staying asleep, and are moody, a little cranky, and crying a lot within the first 2 to 35 days of your baby's birth, don't panic too much, as this may be the usual baby blues. But when this is accompanied by feelings of sadness and any of the other PPD symptoms listed above, then it may be a good idea to speak to a professional to see if you're suffering from PPD. By leaving it unattended, you risk worsening it even more; therefore, to overcome this kind of perinatal depression, you will need to take treatment for it.

Getting help for your PPD will improve your relationship with yourself and your baby. Don't be discouraged by the few people who may not take you seriously at first; this is perfectly normal, since many people, including health-care professionals, aren't educated on the causes and results of conditions like PPD. Instead, keep searching for help until you find someone you can rely on for the support and treatment you need to overcome your condition. And remember that PPD isn't your fault. Therefore, you shouldn't feel any sort of shame or guilt about it.

Accessing Mental Health Resources and Services

A lot of healing, responsibility, and change goes into walking the postpartum journey, and as much as you may want to appear as the supermom who's got it together and going through it like a natural, you still need all the physical, emotional, and mental support you can get. We're often fearful of any complications that may arise after birth, but the complications don't stop once your baby has arrived. PPD is a postpartum complication, so you need a strong support network.

Sometimes, our loved ones and partners may not be too clued in on conditions like PPD. For this reason, it may be a good idea to seek professional help through mental health resources and services. Fortunately, nowadays, you can access these resources and services in person or online, but either way, any option you go for will be of use to you because

- your new journey is highly demanding

- postpartum support can be offered in different ways

- it's easily accessible

- your support system can act as your additional eyes and ears in case you miss anything

- a support network is vital for high-risk babies and moms

Consulting With Therapists and Counselors Who Specialize in Postpartum Mental Health

Professional help can be the best way to work through your PPD and overall mental health. But before you seek the help of a professional, you must keep the following points in mind:

- If you have an insurance plan and intend to use it for therapy, consult with your directory to ensure you're aware of any plan limits you may have. You have the option to see a therapist at your own expense; however, this may be a little expensive.

- Do your research. Instead of hopping on the first health-care professional you find, do some digging to ensure they're a good fit for you. You can always use online reviews to help you find someone online, but you can also get a referral from a doctor, close friend, relative, or colleague.

- Take advantage of mental health organizations that provide mothers like yourself with online databases for finding credible therapists who are licensed and qualified to operate.

- Start locally with resources that can help you find the help you need within your community. This will make it easier and more convenient for you to find the help you need.

- Each therapist specializes in a specific topic relating to mental health; therefore, ensure you find a national association, helpline, or network that addresses PPD.

- Have a clear picture of where you want to be when you start attending your therapy.

- Help won't just come in the form of a professional listening to you each time you're allowed to answer the question, "So, how did that make you feel?" Ask questions so you can make sense of some of the experiences you're going through. Also, before choosing a therapist, find out if they're qualified to provide you with the services you're looking for.

- During therapy sessions, keep a close eye on any red flags you may find. If anything makes you feel uncomfortable, anxious, or uneasy, consider finding help elsewhere, especially if you feel the therapist isn't giving you the help and attention you need.

- Be mindful of how the therapist responds to your concerns. If they interrupt you when you speak, don't keep to time, invalidate your frustrations and concerns, or disrespect you in any way, again, it may be a good idea to consider getting help elsewhere.

There are five main types of health-care professional you can speak to to help you address any concerns you may have regarding PPD. Each of these professionals provides a different service to their customers, so, depending on your needs, contact the one you feel will assist you best:

- **Therapists**: These health-care professionals are more about performing talk therapy and diagnosing mental health conditions like PPD so they can help treat them. Their priority is to provide customers with a safe space to discuss any symptoms, life issues, or changes they may be going through.

- **Psychiatrists**: These health-care professionals help to diagnose and treat mental illnesses, prescribing medications, performing medical tests, and conducting thorough examinations. These professionals pay close attention to biological factors concerning the brain, social sciences, and family histories.

- **Psychologists**: These health-care professionals operate similarly to therapists in performing talk therapy; however, they also go as far as helping clients with issues that aren't necessarily related to mental illnesses. This includes covering issues concerning grief, stress, or major life changes that could significantly impact a patient's life. They also perform examinations and assessments to help get a proper diagnosis of what a patient could be suffering from.

- **Social workers**: These health-care professionals are found in places like hospitals, schools, and mental health facilities, where they work with different kinds of people to provide them with the guidance they need to lead happy and healthy lives. They also coach individuals by encouraging them to use communication, organizational techniques, empathy, skills in self-care, and compassion to improve their lives.

- **Counselors**: These health-care professionals facilitate talk therapy, provide diagnosis, and help treat different mental health conditions. Usually, these professionals will specialize in a specific approach within therapy, and sometimes team up with a medical doctor to offer a more well-rounded strategy for therapy.

A Mental Health Red Flag Checklist for First-Time Moms

Are you worried you may be suffering from possible PPD? Well, here's a quick checklist that you can use to spot some red flags as a first-time mom:

- Your "baby blues" phase hasn't seemed to improve.

- Guilt and sadness are the only ideas that are constantly flooding your mind.

- You no longer enjoy the things you used to take an interest in.

- You're undecided a majority of the time.

- You're always concerned about whether or not you're a good mother to your child.

- You're no longer able to maintain your regular sleep routine.

- You feel like your new journey is big and stressful.

- You often have thoughts of harming yourself.

If you said yes to two or more of these points, then it may be a good idea to speak to a health-care professional.

Next Steps

Our emotions can be caused by our physical state as well as the quality of our thoughts. In the next chapter, you'll learn how to work with your emotions and thoughts to boost your overall resilience.

Chapter Four

EMOTIONAL WELLBEING

*I am a human being, with feelings and emotions and scars and
flaws, just like anyone else.*

Josh Gordon

T he emotional well-being of a new mom is directly affected by changing hormones and thoughts of being overwhelmed, guilty, tired, and
more. In all we do, we must remember that there's also the risk of baby
blues and postpartum depression to watch out for. This chapter explains
the emotional landscape and shares much-needed tools for new moms.

Understanding Postpartum Emotional Changes

We now have a proper understanding of what "baby blues" are and how
they affect you after childbirth in terms of having you run through constant episodes of crying spells, anxiety, mood swings, and a hard time
sleeping for the first two weeks of your postpartum journey. We also know
that once the baby blues go beyond the two-week mark, this could be a

sign of postpartum depression, as your baby blues could be much more severe than you think. But overall, we now know it's important to note that depression can also begin during pregnancy. This is known as peripartum depression. Should your PPD become something like a more extreme case of mood swings, this is known as postpartum psychosis, which, like PPD, develops after the birth of your child.

Learning all there is to know about the emotional changes during your postpartum journey helps you better understand why you feel and think the way you do. It also helps you get the guidance and support you need to overcome any conditions you may be suffering from instead of drowning in silence over the emotional challenges you're going through after childbirth.

Postpartum Depression—An Understanding of Our Emotional Changes After Giving Birth

PPD isn't the only form of depression that new mothers go through after the birth of their child. We typically characterize postpartum depression as symptoms like chronic fatigue, anxiety, and the hopeless feeling of sadness that leaves us trapped in our own mental space. However, PPD has many other symptoms that can affect new mothers, which is why medical professionals have categorized each condition into a specific type of PPD.

Each type of PPD has its own risk factors, progressions, treatment plans, and signs and symptoms, but the important thing to note is that each is classified according to its severity (*Facts About Postpartum Depression*, n.d.).

Postpartum Blues

The postpartum blues are the famous "baby blues" that we've been talking about. This is a short-term form of PPD that's pretty common among postpartum mothers. According to research, 50–85% of postpartum mothers are affected by postpartum blues; however, this type of PPD is different from postpartum depression in the sense that it doesn't necessarily affect a mother's ability to take care of herself and her newborn baby (*Facts About Postpartum Depression*, n.d.). Because its symptoms usually wear off within two weeks or so, medical professionals consider this a normal part of most postpartum journeys. Therefore, it isn't necessarily considered PPD since it isn't as serious as the other types of PPD that we'll be discussing next.

Postpartum Anxiety

Postpartum anxiety is another type of PPD that's also pretty common among postpartum mothers; however, medical professionals find it slightly challenging to diagnose since it's normal for mothers to develop a sense of anxiety around their parenting journey. This explains why we rarely hear mothers saying they suffer from postpartum anxiety, since some of the symptoms are considered an almost "expected" part of life as a new mom. The anxiety becomes serious when it is so severe that it affects how you live your life and ultimately leads to depression. Here, symptoms may include

- fears and worries that feel persistent and can't seem to go away

- suffering from high levels of stress and tension

- finding it difficult to relax

Like the baby blues, postpartum anxiety can be somewhat mild and short term. It should only become a concern when the feelings of severe anxiety go on for longer than two weeks.

Postpartum Obsessive-Compulsive Disorder

About 3–5% of postpartum mothers are affected by obsessive-compulsive disorder (OCD), a mood disorder that's always connected to high levels of anxiety (Pelham, 2023). Here, women have persistent fears about inadvertently harming or killing their baby, driving compulsive habits such as changing their baby over and over again or cleaning repeatedly during the day.

Like postpartum anxiety, there isn't a lot of awareness regarding postpartum OCD. This is because not a lot of mothers will come forth to confess that they've had thoughts about harming or murdering their babies. As women who experience this condition have a great deal of shame and embarrassment about their behaviors and thoughts, it's difficult for medical experts to develop any diagnosis or treatment for the condition.

Postpartum Panic Disorder

Postpartum mood disorder is another form of PPD and occurs in roughly 4–10% of mothers soon after birth (*The Basics of Postpartum Panic Disorder*, 2023). Characterized by high levels of anxiety, mothers with postpartum panic disorder typically find themselves experiencing frequent panic attacks in addition to other symptoms like

- shortness of breath

- episodes of consistent fear and worry

- heart palpitations

- a tight feeling in the chest

Usually, the mood disorder will cause mothers to develop a great sense of fear surrounding death, going crazy, or not being in control of a situation. Suppose you already have thyroid dysfunction, a history of panic attacks, and severe anxiety. In that case, you'll likely be part of the population of from this condition.

Postpartum Post-Traumatic Stress Disorder

Postpartum post-traumatic stress disorder (PTSD) is a unique type of PPD that affects more than 9% of women who've given birth (*Postpartum Post-Traumatic Stress Disorder,* 2021). Usually, mothers who have experienced a great deal of trauma and threat during or after the birth of their baby have PTSD. Usually, these traumatic events include

- a birth complication

- having your baby go to the neonatal intensive care unit (NICU) immediately after birth

- having to undergo an emergency C-section

- suffering from birth injuries

Women who have also suffered other previous traumatic experiences, like violence, abuse, or sexual assault, may also develop PTSD after giving birth. To spot the condition, you should look out for symptoms like

- constantly reliving the traumatic moment through different memories and flashbacks

- doing your best to avoid any triggers that may remind you of the traumatic event

- constantly experiencing panic attacks and high levels of anxiety

- having trouble sleeping

- irritability

- feeling disconnected, unavailable, or numb from your physical reality

Self-blame, shame, and guilt are common emotions that many postpartum mothers experience when they suffer from PTSD. Even if something could have been done to change the situation, letting go and making the decision to move forward can be the best thing you can do for yourself.

Postpartum Psychosis

Postpartum psychosis is the most severe form of PPD, but, fortunately, it's a rare mood disorder affecting one mother out of every 1,000 births (*Postpartum Depression Types*, 2023). As with PPD, those who suffer from the condition usually display symptoms during the first two weeks after giving birth; this includes displaying behaviors like

- hallucinations

- confusion

- having delusional thoughts

- hyperactivity

- being unable to make sound judgments

- extreme agitation

A postpartum mother who's suffering from postpartum psychosis will usually behave the same way a person with bipolar disorder would. It's worth noting that if you have a history of bipolar disorder, it's likely that you'll develop postpartum psychosis. If you're concerned you may have the condition, it's best to seek professional help so you can receive immediate attention, treatment, and support. Looking after a baby while experiencing postpartum psychosis can be very dangerous as women often find themselves unconscious of their behavior and actions. There have been cases of women harming or killing themselves or their newborn babies because of the condition. Therefore, it's crucial to not take it lightly.

Common Emotional Challenges Faced by New Mothers

Motherhood can involve a roller coaster of emotions. Fortunately, by understanding what happens to your body before, during, and after birth, you begin to see that these highs and lows are pretty common among all mothers. So, to comfort you on this journey, common emotional challenges that we're all at risk of facing as first-time moms include

- postpartum depression

- anxiety

- guilt

- stress

- isolation and loneliness

- a loss of identity

- feeling sleep deprived

Embracing and Expressing Emotions

By normalizing the range of emotions that we, as first-time moms, experience, we can comfort one another, embrace our journey, and become comfortable enough to express our true emotions.

With services like acceptance and commitment therapy (ACT), postpartum mothers can develop a healthy relationship with their emotions by accepting the journey they're currently on while choosing to commit to habits that align with their vision and values. In embracing the fact that challenging feelings and thoughts are a part of life that we can't run away from, we accept all the milestones and hiccups that we encounter along the way. Through ACT, first-time moms are encouraged to exercise value-based behavioral patterns, self-compassion, and mindfulness to help them achieve a meaningful, intentional, and fulfilling life. This allows mothers to become more content and find some gratitude for the path they're currently walking.

Mindfulness and self-compassion are great ways to embrace and express your emotions. With mindfulness, you're choosing to become intentional about paying close attention to every sensation in your body, your emotions, and your thoughts. As you do this, the goal is to not be hard on yourself or judge the different things you notice. Instead, by being more conscious of your emotions, you're able to validate yourself on purpose and respond constructively if you feel there's a thought you would like to change. Then, with self-compassion, you use understanding and kindness to address any weaknesses and mistakes you find in yourself. The goal is to turn into your own best friend so you don't criticize yourself or beat yourself up over past experiences that you can no longer change. By exercising compassion toward yourself, you're able to reassure yourself and create the safe space you'd want someone else to give you if you opened up to them about the emotional struggles you're facing.

Once you combine self-compassion and mindfulness with value-based intentions, you ensure your decisions align with your goals and values. Regardless of what you are going through at the time, value-based intentions help you achieve a great sense of fulfillment and purpose. With all three of these components, you afford yourself the safe space you need to

- validate and express your emotions

- engage with your emotions

- manage your emotional challenges

- take care of your needs

- use art, journaling, and other creative outlets to express and release your emotions

Nurturing an Emotional Connection WithYourself

Earning the "Supermom of the Year" trophy is great, but getting the title doesn't mean pretending to have it all together while you suffer on the inside. Being a first-time mom means this is a journey you've never walked before, and every day will likely come with something new. Knowing this, it's healthy to ask for help and support in your time of need while eliminating thoughts that suggest

- nobody will want to help you if you speak up about your emotional needs

- you're playing weak

- soon enough, you and your baby will turn into burdens

- you're doing something wrong because most mothers seem to be doing fine

Seeking emotional help can be challenging because we often feel like our outbursts or moments of vulnerability or weakness may be taken the wrong way, rejected, or turned into a joke. And because there's not a lot of awareness of the emotional challenges mothers go through during the postpartum phase, there's very little understanding of this time in your life. But instead of "dying on the inside," perhaps it's time you start looking into ways to establish open and honest emotional connections with loved ones.

Seeking Emotional Support Through Open and Honest Communication

Before heading off to a therapist or deciding to join a postpartum support group to be part of a community of other mothers who share similar interests, why not consider trying to establish a relationship of emotional support with your loved ones? Because of how misinformed most people are on the postpartum journey, you can find ways to express your emotions through effective communication. Yes, this will be a little challenging at first, but it's important to remember that you interact with your loved ones constantly. Without a proper way to express yourself, you'll likely feel frustrated, angry, and stressed toward them for not "trying to understand where you're coming from." So, to nurture your close relationships and create a safe space for you to be open and honest about your emotions and needs, you can initiate the communication channels by

- figuring out the kind of support you need so you know what to ask for when the time arrives for you to be open and honest about your emotional needs

- attempting to remove any existing barriers like feelings, assumptions, and ideas that may be standing between you and the support you're looking for

- only seeking emotional support from people you trust and know will be emotionally available for you

- being assertive about articulating your needs

- always showing appreciation for the support others give you

- availing yourself emotionally when others also need you

In conjunction with getting the emotional support you need from loved ones, you can supplement this with other alternatives like joining postpartum support groups or online communities that you believe will also assist you in getting the help you need.

Managing Stress and Anxiety

In an attempt to respond to a traumatic event, major challenge, or threat, our bodies release the hormones we need to take action. This is known as stress. We all respond to stress differently; however, there are common fight-or-flight responses that most of us experience when we're stressed. These include

- an increased heart rate

- feeling of concern

- insecurity regarding yourself and the environment you're in

- thoughts of a way forward

Stress, fear, and anxiety are all negative emotions that we all feel naturally. Of course, when they overwhelm you to the point of limiting how you can live your life, this will come off as unhealthy; however, truthfully, these negative emotions are designed to keep us safe from various threats and harms.

When we're triggered into feeling stressed, that reality immediately tells us what we're up against; this allows us to quickly know what we're capable of internally rather than having to live up to what we project. Each time we're able to spot our stress triggers, it allows us to become more self-aware and mindful of our actions and choices.

Stress can come from various places and be caused by different things. When you're able to identify your stress triggers, you can immediately work on understanding their root causes. Therefore, to help you understand this, let's look at the three types of stress triggers:

- **Routine stress:** This comes from our daily lives, such as always managing heavy workloads, what goes on at home, and other commitments that we face regularly.

- **Disruptive change:** Life's changes can sometimes increase our stress levels because we see them as disruptions to what we're used to. So, disruptive changes can come from moving to a new place, attending a new school, or starting a new job.

- **Traumatic events:** Accidents, abuse, and loss are extreme triggers that cause stress. With no real way to cure or erase the pain we hold within, it's pretty difficult to develop a definitive way of handling PTSD.

Discomfort, unpleasant life experiences, previous traumatic events, and the social support you have all contribute to pushing you to become stressed. But in learning to manage and cope with these stress and anxiety triggers, you must first know how to identify them. This involves

- always monitoring your physical health

- being conscious of how your job makes you feel

- evaluating everything that's going on in your life

- not entertaining situations you have no control over

Implementing Stress Management Techniques

Because stress isn't something we can eliminate, we need to adopt tech-niques to help us manage it. If your anxiety and stress levels are always high and out of control, speaking to a professional may be a good idea. However, there are some techniques you can apply at home each time you're triggered into feeling stressed. These include

- calming yourself down to help you lower your blood pressure

- chewing gum, as the rhythmic act of chewing helps reduce stress levels and ease tension in the body

- going outside for some fresh air

- keeping a genuine smile on your face, because the muscles around your mouth reduce stress responses in the body

- inhaling lavender-scented oils to ease your stress while soothing your body

- listening to your favorite music

- focusing on your breath by engaging in various breathing exercises

- exercising compassion and kindness toward yourself

- journaling as honestly and often as you can

- confiding in a close friend

- trying to find ways to be more productive

- adopting a positive mindset and attitude

- coming to terms with the fact that you should let go of things you have no control over

- choosing to address issues assertively and not aggressively

- managing your time effectively

- establishing boundaries and limits

- creating time for the things you enjoy and love

- avoiding alcohol, compulsive behaviors, and drugs as distractions that you rely on to ease your stress

- seeking social support

- seeking different treatments that you can use to manage any mental health conditions you may be suffering from

- exercising, including any form of light, moderate, or intense physical activity

- maintaining a healthy and balanced diet

- getting quality sleep

- engaging in relaxation techniques like breathing exercises and meditation

- connecting with others, your behavior, and your inner voice

Next Steps

A lot of focus is given to the mother–baby bond, but there are a lot of misconceptions about it too. We'll explore the myths and the facts in the next chapter.

Chapter Five

MOTHER AND BABY

Personally, becoming a mother has been such a rewarding and wonderful experience. However, at times it has also been a huge challenge. Even for me who has support at home that most mothers do not. Nothing can prepare you for the sheer overwhelming experience of what it means to become a mother. It is full of complex emotions of joy, exhaustion, love, and worry, all mixed. Your fundamental identity changes overnight.

Kate Middleton

Developing secure attachments and fostering a maternal bond with a newborn is vital for the child's emotional well-being and long-term development. The goal is for parents to gain practical knowledge and strategies to promote secure attachment, interpret and respond to their baby's cues, and nurture a strong and nurturing bond with their newborn. So, this chapter is dedicated to helping you create the bond you and your baby need to build a meaningful relationship.

What Is Newborn Attachment and Maternal Bonding?

Aside from doing the daily work of feeding, bathing, changing, burping, and attending to your baby's needs, there's the actual relationship you also need to build between you and your newborn baby. This is known as the newborn attachment and maternal bonding part of your motherhood journey.

Attachment Versus Bonding

Each time you connect with your baby, it's important to ensure both your needs are met. This explains the attachment theory and bonding theory. The newborn attachment theory simply describes the bond that a baby will build with their primary caregiver; the maternal bonding theory describes the behaviors, thoughts, and feelings the primary caregiver will build with the baby. It may sound a little confusing to imagine a newborn baby making any effort to build a relationship; however, this will make sense to you as we move through the chapter.

The Importance of Bonding Time

As well as handling your baby physically, you'll want to ensure you're connecting with your baby each time you hold them. Mothers who can instantly connect with their babies right after birth are fortunate in that regard. But if you haven't established that bond as yet, there's no need to worry because it's perfectly normal. Many mothers are unable to connect with their little ones during pregnancy and, because the birth process is physically and mentally intense, they may respond a little differently just minutes, hours, or days after birth. The good news is that you can do something about it.

Physical closeness can do wonders in helping you establish a special emotional connection with your baby. Every mother will choose her own way to display this physical closeness, but the important thing is to be intentional about your effort to fall in love with your baby. Bonding with your newborn baby is great for their development, because children desire to be shown love and affection from a very early age.

Establishing a bond between you and your baby doesn't only benefit them, as you'll also desire that sort of connection with your child. In addition to self-doubt and the range of negative emotions and thoughts you may be experiencing, feeling as though you have no bond with your baby will often make you believe "my child doesn't love me." Because newborn infants aren't able to like or dislike anyone yet, this sort of idea is rather unhealthy to entertain. But feeling like you and your baby don't have a bond will affect the relationship you have with your little one: Each time they cry uncontrollably or go quiet and calm when they're in the arms of someone else, these unhealthy ideas will make you feel like motherhood isn't for you. And that's not true.

When it comes to handling and holding your baby, you can work on bonding by focusing on soothing and skin-to-skin techniques. With skin-to-skin techniques, you create a physical skin-to-skin bond with your baby by holding them against your bare chest in an upright position. Whether they're calm or restless, this technique helps to

- regulate your baby's heart rate and temperature

- regulate your baby's breathing

- assist your little one in adapting to their new life outside of the womb

- have the baby's skin become one with your naturally friendly bacteria

- stimulate your baby's digestion

- increase their appetite

When practicing skin-to-skin techniques, you must avoid scented lotions, soaps, and perfumes at all times. The daily skin products we use often contain dyes, herbs, botanicals, chemicals, and fragrances that can affect a baby's breathing and skin (Davis, 2008). Although you will be using unscented products for your baby's skincare, your own skin products may rub off on them, which may result in skin irritation. In addition, avoiding cigarettes and smoking may also make the skin-to-skin techniques a lot more effective.

When you engage in skin-to-skin techniques, be sure to wear comfortable clothes and spend your bonding time in a room that's comfortable and not too bright. Also, have the space you're sitting in be free from any noises and distractions as you gently speak, read, or sing to your little one. They may fall asleep during this time so be sure not to think your efforts weren't effective.

Soothing techniques are additional ways to connect with your baby comfortably and satisfyingly. You can always use skin-to-skin techniques in conjunction with soothing techniques to connect with your little one and enjoy additional benefits that will help with their development. Some of the benefits you can expect to gain from this technique include

- helping your baby relieve any crying and stress

- improving your baby's sleep routine

Massage, sounds, and swaddling are three of the best soothing techniques. Not only are they infant friendly, but methods like sound use are great for stimulating infant hearing. When it comes to swaddling, this method affords newborns the chance to feel comfortable and secure. It's advisable to learn how to swaddle correctly to provide the comfort your baby needs. If you don't do it correctly, you risk wrapping your baby so tightly that it becomes uncomfortable for them to breathe. Also, swaddling isn't ideal for babies that can roll over, as it risks their lives by exposing them to sudden infant death syndrome (SIDS).

Common Bonding Myths That Are Far From True

Parent–child bonding is often defined pretty vaguely. This explains why numerous misconceptions exist about what certain behaviors mean when a child treats a parent in a certain way. Of course, children are sensitive to negative energy and tension; however, most parents don't take it too well when they feel they're unable to establish a bond with their child. With the baby blues and PPD already on a high, you may feel further self-doubt when you watch your little one warm up to others, cry for long periods when they're with you, or perhaps not want to be held by you when someone else enters the room. Some may laugh this off, but these reactions become a problem when mothers associate their baby's love with the their baby shows affection toward them. So, let's look at common myths you shouldn't give any thought to whenever you're attempting to bond with your little one.

Babies Don't Recall People and Experiences

Part of bonding with your newborn baby means keeping their physical environment consistent. Granted, circumstances may force us to sometimes move our little ones around from time to time, but try to avoid moving your little ones from one space to the next all the time. During the first two years of a child's life, their development is at a critical stage, meaning each event and environment you expose them to will form their lifelong attitude on who and what to trust. By changing their environments and the people they're exposed to regularly, you risk putting them in a position of feeling they're not lovable, since babies feel the same—if not more intense—emotions adults feel when they're separated from what they're used to.

A Child Will Always Behave the Same

Sometimes, you'll find babies who are a lot more sociable and easy-going than others. When they're among others, they seem like infants who are good at bonding; when this happens a few times, you may assume they'll behave the same when they're exposed to other and more people. While this can make it easy for you to bring your child with you when you're in the company of others, it's important not to believe that children love or bond with people generically. When you believe this, you assume they aren't sensitive to different people and spaces, which is untrue.

If your child can form emotional connections with specific people and environments, this is a healthy way of bonding. Understand that establishing any sort of relationship with someone else will require time and, by respecting that, you train your little one to establish boundaries immediately when they enter new spaces or meet new people.

Believing That Bonding Is a Gift

Unfortunately, the fact that your baby can "cooperate" with you the majority of the time doesn't mean they have some sort of solid bond with you. Some babies are naturally easy-going, but if your little one is a bit fussy at times or quick to express their disapproval, don't sweat it. Like any normal relationship, having a few "disagreements" with your little one is common, since all relationships have their ups and downs from time to time.

Many mothers believe their children don't like them if they find them to be quite fussy or agitated each time they're with them. This is especially the case when their father or someone else who's close to them happens to enter the room and the baby suddenly changes and becomes calmer. When this happens often, it may make you feel you're doing something wrong. It may even make you feel like someone else is shifting the attention off you and becoming the favorite with your baby that you're hoping to be. But don't worry—because bonding with your child isn't something you can train your child to do, since no one has conscious control over it, afford yourself and your baby enough time alone to create a natural bond that will gradually grow with time.

Gluing Yourself to Your Baby Will Grow the Bond

Yes, spending quality time with your little one does play a significant role in helping establish a strong bond between you and your baby. This knowledge may be great during the first few weeks of your postpartum journey; however, you may lose trust in your bond once you prepare to head back to work, since you'll begin to believe that not spending time with your baby or being physically distant from them will somehow destroy the bond you've already established.

The number of hours you spend with a baby won't guarantee you'll develop a bond with them. In other words, if you have a bond with your child already and it's managed to grow strong because you've been spending a lot of time together, attending to other commitments like work or your social life won't affect that already-existing bond. A child usually bonds with their primary caregiver, and even when you start going out to work again, when you return home to spend quality time with your baby they won't have a sudden change of heart toward you. So, ensure the time you spend with your baby is quality time that involves the two of you bonding and interacting with each other.

The Newborn–Parent Bond

Babies spend a lot of their time watching and listening to the people and sounds around them. During this time, they also begin to register who makes the regular effort to entertain, soothe, feed, and comfort them, and attend to their every need. This becomes a routine to them, and, within the first three months of their birth, they'll start to play around with different grins, grimaces, and other body movements that will express their approval, disapproval, friendliness, and pleasure.

Babies do a lot to exercise various parts of their bodies and muscles. Even something as simple as a smile is a major turning point for them, because, by moving their lips, they are trying to establish some sort of conversation with you. This could mean they're happy, trying to express a need, or attempting to exert some sort of control. From time to time, your little one may even go as far as imitating some of the facial expressions or movements they see you doing. It's good to encourage your baby to play around with different parts of their bodies like their hands and feet, because this advances their brain development and moves them away from focusing too much on internal sensations that may cause them discomfort, like gas. Plus, the more you interact and socialize with your baby, the more they'll become familiar with different experiences and environments.

As you work on trying to establish a bond with your baby, pay attention to what needs they're trying to communicate with you. Sometimes, we get a little caught up in trying to build a routine. We also try to schedule activities and needs according to our own timetables. But in the first three months of your postpartum journey, don't be too quick to work on routines. Use this time to work on connecting with your baby and attending to the needs they're communicating. You can do this by

- immediately responding to urgent needs that suggest they're hungry or in pain

- interpreting signs like peaceful sleep or attempts to entertain or alert themselves as proof that you've met all your baby's needs

- exercising patience when you find your little one a tad fussy and restless even after meeting all their obvious needs

By using these first three months to learn about your baby and the different ways they'll communicate their needs, you can then develop personalized responses to respond to those needs. For instance, when they cry after feeding them and changing their diaper, perhaps they need a bit of soothing. By now, you'll know which positions to hold or rock them in so they can calm down and enjoy the soothing experience that they need. During this time, it's important to exercise a lot of patience with your baby. Babies don't always use smiles, gestures, and different facial expressions to communicate their needs. Sometimes, they may use crying as a way to communicate their needs. This will be a little frustrating for you, but remember to remain calm and patient at all times.

Secure Attachment Through Sensitive and Responsive Caregiving

Through sensitive and responsive caregiving, you can secure a healthy attachment to your baby—and this will go both ways. There are numerous strategies you can use to achieve this, but in every effort you make, ensure you remain

- consistent

- responsive

- encouraging

- understanding

With an understanding of the different ways your baby will communicate their needs to you, you can use secure attachment methods to exercise empathy, emotional well-being, self-regulation, and behavior that encourages them to socialize and interact with you. To do this, you need to ensure you're

- showing empathy and sensitivity by remaining consistent, responsible, and caring each time they try to communicate something to you—over time, this will develop into trust

- responding calmly by modeling calm behavior that suggests you're in control of your emotions—newborn babies feed off your energy a lot of the time, so if you react explosively, they'll likely do the same

- showing you're involved in whatever experience you're having at the time by being present and choosing to interact with your baby in a positive and engaging way

- continuously showing your nurturing side through positive behavior like maintaining eye contact, laughing, using facial expressions that suggest you're calm, and touching your baby in a kind and gentle way—in all you do, show them that you're interested in them and that you're committed to developing a sense of security and attachment

Early Interactions and Emotional Connection

Some mothers can establish an instant connection with their newborn babies, while others may take a bit of time. But if you find yourself feeling slightly disconnected from your little one, don't beat yourself up about it, because it's perfectly normal. Fortunately, all hope is not lost when it comes to building any sort of bond with your baby, because you can always try different interactions and emotional connections to establish or strengthen your bond.

The Importance of Physical Touch With Newborn Babies

Physical touch plays a significant role in helping you form a strong bond with your newborn baby. You can always speak to a nurse or your midwife about the different ways you can connect with your baby in this way, but it's important to be gentle and take your time. Because this isn't a rushed process that's just a quick in and out, you want to ensure you're

- dressed comfortably

- placing your little one on your chest in a comfortable way and position for both of you

- covering your baby to keep them snuggled, warm, and comfortable

- relaxed

You're about to have an intimate moment with your baby; therefore, you want to ensure you keep the following points in mind:

- Avoid having any electronic devices or gadgets lying around as these will cause a distraction and keep you away from focusing on your baby.

- Avoid placing your baby on skin that may have a rash, cold sores, or open cuts. Ensure your skin is always healthy, clean, and free of any fragrances at all times.

- Avoid smoking before or during your sessions of physical touch.

- Avoid physical touch if you're ill.

Like with adults, physical touch can be a great love language to use on your baby, especially because babies aren't yet at an age where they can understand any verbal or emotional expressions. Plus, you're a little limited in how far you can go when it comes to physical expressions, since newborn babies aren't physically big enough to accept hugs, cuddling, or shoulder squeezes.

Through kissing, gentle massage, rubbing their hands and feet, and skin-to-skin touching, you can explore different ways of physically touching your baby to connect with them in the best way possible. During these intimate moments, your little one's body will release a hormone known as oxytocin, which will make them feel good. When they're in their feel-good moment, you'll trigger all kinds of physical touch benefits that include

- stabilizing your newborn's heart rate

- improving their breathing pattern

- encouraging healthy sleep

- supporting physical growth

- relieving any pains your little one may be experiencing at the time

- reducing your child's risk of getting a serious infection, developing hypothermia, or dying

Physical touch can be a steady and effective way to build a bond with your baby. Also, when you work on comforting your baby this way, your body responds positively, increasing your milk supply and helping you feel confident in knowing you're taking good care of your baby and attending to their every need.

Skin-to-Skin Contact—A Great Form of Physical Touch

Skin-to-skin contact, also known as "kangaroo care," is an effective way of establishing physical contact with your baby. Here, you'll hold your little one against your chest while ensuring there's skin-to-skin contact between the two of you. This is a special experience that's helped many postpartum mothers bond with their babies while enjoying a number of medical benefits, including

- improving your baby's physical health

- increasing your milk supply

- nurturing the bond that you're helping to create

The Significance of Eye Contact and Facial Expressions in Bonding

As well as physical touch, communication and conversation are key in creating a bond between yourself and your newborn baby. This is where eye contact and positive facial expressions come into play. Without needing to verbally communicate anything with your baby, you can use these techniques to let your baby know

- you're being sincere, honest, and caring in that moment

- you understand the message your baby is trying to communicate

- you're confident in what you're doing

Eye contact is a great way to reveal any thoughts and feelings you want to share with your baby. We may think our babies are unable to understand our facial expressions and what we're trying to tell them during eye contact; however, this isn't true. When we feel a certain way about something, our brains trigger certain neurons, and the same thing happens in another person's brain if they happen to be watching us when we experience that emotion; this is because of mirror neurons that exist in our bodies (Stacy, 2019). Our babies are equally sensitive to our facial expressions and eye contact.

Understanding the Importance of a Caregiver's Responsiveness

Crying, facial expressions, and body language are the different ways in which your newborn baby will communicate with you. Even if you've already attended to their basic needs, it's always important to respond. I've come across many mothers who deliberately choose to pretend they can't hear their children communicate with them, especially when they're crying, because they believe it will teach them a sense of independence while helping them learn to self-soothe. There are various ways you can teach your child to self-soothe and gain independence; however, ignoring your baby's signals only makes them feel you aren't willing to listen to what they're trying to tell you regarding their needs. Validating them in the way they need grows your bond and establishes trust.

Do all you can to talk to your baby as often as possible, even when they're quiet. This will help them identify you by your face, personal scent, and voice. So, as you talk to them more and more, be sure to

- speak slowly

- use soft tones to say what you want to say

- let your baby know what you're telling them is for them by using a voice that's high-pitched and soft

- sing along to songs

- use short sentences or single words to speak to them

- call your little one by their name

- repeat the sounds or words that make your little one laugh and smile

Overcoming Guilt and Self-Doubt to Strengthen the Maternal Bond

Mom guilt is part of almost everyone's motherhood journey. It's usually associated with feelings of shame and guilt when you compare the efforts you make as a mother to the efforts other mothers seemingly make toward their children. It's an internal dialogue that goes on in your mind where, essentially, every thought is centered around you feeling like a failure as a mother.

Unfortunately, mom guilt is an experience most mothers go through and, although you may think you aren't doing enough as a mother, the reason these feelings and thoughts come up isn't entirely tied to your abilities as a mother. There are underlying issues that cause you to feel that way, which usually include

- having low self-esteem

- not being stable mentally

- using negative coping mechanisms to deal with difficult situations

- spreading yourself thin by trying to "do it all"

- allowing social media to build your picture of what a "good mom" looks like

With so much now taking us away from being the traditional mother who stays at home all the time to attend to her child's needs, mothers who suffer from any of the points mentioned above can often feel a heavy sense of guilt and shame when they do any of the following:

- struggling to produce enough breastmilk, or considering not breastfeeding

- being a working mom who has to return to work after her maternity break

- not working outside the home, and feeling a sense of guilt for not being able to independently provide for your child

- feeling bored when you need to look after your newborn baby

- using screen time as a distraction for your baby

- asking for help

- feeling like you aren't spending enough time with your baby

- allowing those close to you to judge you

- losing your temper

- comparing yourself with other mothers

- suffering from PPD

How to Overcome Guilt and Self-Doubt

Whenever you find yourself experiencing any sort of mom guilt, follow these 10 steps to help you overcome it

1. Take a moment to take a deep breath.

2. Ask yourself what the source of your guilt and shame could be.

3. Exercise self-compassion on yourself.

4. Challenge the negative thoughts you have about yourself.

5. Indulge in a bit of self-care.

6. In a quiet space, pay attention to what your intuition is saying.

7. Look at your social circle and only surround yourself with people who inspire, support, and empower you.

8. Take time off if you feel you need to.

9. Try seeking professional help if you feel you're truly struggling with intense emotions of guilt and shame.

10. Give conscious parenting a try.

Understanding Attachment Theory

When we talk about understanding what an attachment is, we're simply talking about the deep emotional bond that we and our newborn babies develop by trying to find a closeness and sense of security between the two of us. Years ago, a man by the name of John Bowlby developed a concept known as "attachment theory," which was initially used back in the 950s to treat children who were troubled emotionally (Mcleod, 2023). While studying the psychological significance of how a child's relationship with their mother influences their cognitive, emotional, and social development, he began to understand why children turn out the way they do when they lack any sort of connection to their mother.

While studying this connection, he came up with four types of attachment styles that describe the impact of how a child is brought upon how they ultimately relate to different relationships and the children they one day raise themselves. A child's early experiences are the foundation of how they will seek comfort, protection, and support during their times of need.

The Four Types of Attachment Style

Secure Attachment

With secure attachments, a child can establish secure and stable relationships with others. Each time they're faced with a challenging situation, they respond healthily. This type of attachment is characterized by trust, a sense of belonging, and feeling worthy of love.

Anxious Attachment

A child with an anxious attachment will typically become overly concerned about whether those they care for will reciprocate their desire to be loved and cared for. When a child is raised by a parent who isn't consistent in responding to the needs they communicate, and who isn't reliable, this later develops into an anxious attachment when they're older and establishing relationships with others.

Avoidant Attachment

When a child is raised to avoid any sort of interaction with their mother, this will later turn into an avoidant attachment. Here, the child is trained to not show any sort of distress, panic, or concern toward their mother during episodes of separation; this could be because the mother ignored any attempts the baby would make to be intimate. This then teaches the child to not depend on their mother for any sort of support. When the child grows up, they will display the same lack of dependence on others.

Fearful Attachment

Children who don't identify with secure, anxious, or avoidant attachments usually fall into the category of having a fearful attachment. Here, the child will usually display behavioral patterns in line with not having any goals or intentions. When a mother displays any sort of frightened behavior in front of their child, and the child is expected to rely on the same person the mother is afraid of, this creates a great sense of confusion in the child. This then causes the child to have a fearful attachment.

The Different Stages of Attachment

When you look at a baby for the first year or 18 months of their life, you discover that they go through different stages of attachment. These include the following:

- **The asocial stage:** This stage occurs between birth and the first six weeks of a baby's life. During this time, a newborn baby's reactions to social and nonsocial stimuli will turn into a response in the form of a smile or other expression.

- **The indiscriminate stage:** This stage occurs between the first six weeks and seven months of a child's life. Here, the baby will show they're enjoying the company of others, so they'll respond in a disapproving way if someone they'd been spending time with leaves. To express their comfort and familiarity with someone, they'll smile or pull other facial expressions to show they're happy with who they're with.

- **The specific stage:** This stage occurs between the first seven and nine months of a child's life. During this time, a child will have a special preference for a specific individual, because they'll be looking for someone who always makes them feel safe, comfortable, and secure. Each time this special person leaves, they'll develop separation anxiety and have a fear of people they don't know.

- **The multiple attachment stage:** This stage starts from the age of 10 months and progresses throughout the child's life. Here, a child will start attaching to multiple people at one time, such as their mother, father, siblings, and grandparents, since their sense of independence is growing.

To have your child develop secure attachments toward yourself and others, you must foster their emotional well-being while creating a space and environment for them to grow through every one of the different stages of attachment healthily. Eventually, they'll develop their sense of independence and establish healthy relationships with others.

Challenges to Bonding and Attachment

Denying your baby a bonding experience, repeated rejection, unsafe and chaotic environments, neglect, and abuse are the main factors that contribute to a child struggling to have any sort of bond and attachment with their mother. To overcome this, mothers need to look within and work on addressing these factors. This includes working on any personal challenges you may be experiencing as well, like stress, anxiety, and PPD. If you're struggling to work on these challenges yourself and aren't sure of how to go about it, don't be afraid to reach out to professional healthcare providers who will give you the help and support you need. Remember that you aren't alone in this and that many mothers are likely in a similar situation to yours. Your child matters, so do all you can to assure them they have the protection, security, and affection they need.

Bonding Activities and Rituals for Mothers and New-borns

The affection you give your baby should always be warm and gentle so your baby feels safe and connected to you. With this in mind, you can engage in bonding activities and rituals that involve

- stroking your little one gently each time you bathe them, change their diaper, or put them down in their bed

- responding to your baby's cries using any of the responses we discussed previously

- holding your baby, including skin-to-skin contact

- supporting your baby's head and neck each time you hold them

- wrapping your baby against you while doing chores or attending to something

- talking to your baby as often as possible

- singing different songs to your baby

- making eye contact with your child each time you sing, talk, or make a facial expression

Next Steps

Letting go of social pressures, expectations, and your attachment to how parents "should" be will help you enjoy the experience more. We'll explore how you can achieve this in the next chapter.

Chapter Six

DON'T SWEAT THE SMALL STUFF

In the age of social media, when you can edit your life in beautiful pictures, it's important to remind moms that all of us are wearing yogurt and all of our hands smell like urine.

Kristen Bell

We often put ourselves and those around us under a lot of pressure as we gradually work on embracing our postpartum journey. But this only frustrates us and those who may be trying to offer us the support and help we need. So, instead of promoting the idea of having you tell everyone, "Get used to it," I'll be showing you how you can relieve yourself of this pressure and find more effective ways to channel your frustrations.

Myths and Misconceptions About Being a New Mom

Many misconceptions float around about first-time mothers who are navigating through their postpartum journey, and most people make a complete joke about it. However, with clear knowledge of why we struggle so much in our journey and how damaging our challenges can be, and by understanding where we are physically, emotionally, and mentally, we can find effective ways to manage our paths while educating those around us on how they can support us in the best way possible. But before we can get into any other stuff, let's quickly iron out some myths and misconceptions that need to be cleared up:

- You're a good mother if you can always tell what your baby needs when they need it.

- Holding your baby too much will delay their independence.

- Always trust your maternal instincts.

- If it isn't "love at first sight," you're doing something wrong.

- Gentle parenting will make room for your child to take advantage of you.

- Introducing your child to fruits first will likely make them dislike vegetables.

- Babies should be potty-trained as soon as possible.

- Breastfeeding is the only way you can truly bond with your child.

- There's a set age at which your child should be walking and talking.

- To make a child smarter, you should read to them every day.

- Your depressed emotions will automatically soak into your little one, making them feel the same way.

- Breastfeeding is easy.

- Seeking help and support for PPD will lead you to lose custody of your child.

- A new addition to the family always brings the family, your marriage, or your relationship closer.

- Babies cry all the time.

- You'll hardly have the time to take a shower or apply some make-up.

- Your postpartum journey should be about you enjoying your new role while bonding with your child.

- You'll hardly have any time to leave the house.

- It'll be years before you get a proper night's rest.

- You'll hardly have time for your phone.

- Your vagina won't be as "tight" as it used to be.

- It's best to start embracing the reality that your entire world will revolve around your newborn baby.

- You and your spouse will hardly have any time for anything romantic.

- Motherhood is a natural and fulfilling journey that will always bring out the best in you.

- There's a right and wrong way of doing things.

- Moms always know.

Know What's Important to You

Losing yourself in raising a child is a pretty easy thing to do because nurturing a baby is something that comes naturally, even if you don't necessarily acknowledge the "right" and "wrong" way of doing things. While it isn't always good to rely only on your maternal instincts to guide you, you can work on refining those instincts by understanding what's most important to you and staying true to yourself. But how do you do this? How do you identify the personal values that matter most to you? Well, you can get to this by answering the following questions:

- What memories do I have that are most meaningful to me?

- Which memories make me feel the least satisfied?

- Which motivational stories have inspired me so far?

- What upsets me the most?

- What do I desire the most from this experience?

- What have I done so far that's worth recognizing and rewarding?

As you answer each of these questions, use the responses as guidelines for what you value the most. Then, use those values to determine the parenting style you'd like to use on your baby. Sometimes, you may depend on your childhood experiences to guide you as to what's most and least important in parenting; however, it's always good to look within as well, since your preferences may change over time. With everything that either upsets you or leaves you the least satisfied, use that as a guide as to what's the least important to you.

Let Go of Should-Haves, Expectations, and Perfectionism

Trauma, childhood experiences, and negative thought patterns will lead you to points of regret, setting high expectations, and always feeling the need to have everything go according to plan. Instead of inspiring you to do better in areas you feel need improving, should-haves, expectations, and striving for perfectionism only choke you into being critical of yourself all the time. This leads to fear, anxiety, and a lot of self-doubt on your end, while ultimately affecting the way you'll go about your parenting relationship with your child.

Overcoming these qualities can be difficult to do; however, like depression, these are unhealthy traits and ideas to have, because all they do is suffocate and frustrate every relationship you have.

Let Go of Social Pressures, Guilt, and Comparisons

The last thing any mother needs is to feel judged, ridiculed, or belittled. For this reason, many postpartum mothers refrain from opening up to those closest to them or asking for more help and support, because they don't want to appear weak or wrong as a result of the social pressures, guilt, and comparisons that people always make. You being your own jury is already bad enough, so by the time other people assume they're bringing something to your attention, you've likely entertained that thought already since you're questioning yourself every second of the day.

All these negative emotions can leave us feeling unworthy. Over time, this leads to self-doubt. If we don't work on these thoughts and feelings, we drift into a depressive state that leaves us feeling stuck and hopeless.

Next Steps

Your body goes through some massive changes during your postpartum journey. In the next chapter, we'll take a look at how not panicking over all the little things will help prepare you to manage any pressure you may be feeling.

Chapter Seven

THE PHYSICAL AFTERMATH

*I think a woman's body after having a baby is pretty amaz-
ing... You just did the most incredible miracle that life has to
offer. I mean, you gave birth to a human being! So I would like
to see that celebrated.*

Blake Lively

Understanding the physical aftermath of childbirth is crucial for new mothers to navigate their postpartum recovery effectively. From body changes to healing from vaginal or cesarean birth, managing postpartum pain and discomfort, hormonal adjustments, and the importance of rest and nutrition, this knowledge empowers new mothers to prioritize their physical well-being.

Postpartum Body Changes

Postpartum body changes often take many of us by surprise. We're often so focused on the life we're bringing into this world—and what life will be like when that happens—we completely forget about the body changes that we should expect after our baby has arrived. From extra tummy skin and stretch marks to hyperpigmentation and excess weight, there's a lot to get to grips with when it comes to how your body will look and feel after giving birth.

Understanding Hormonal Fluctuations and Their Effects

We've already established that a mother's postpartum body goes through a lot of change. This means going through all sorts of hormonal fluctuations, which explains why we go through the baby blues, and experience being excited and thrilled to be mothers one minute only to go on a downward spiral of negative emotions straight after. During labor, your hormones are at an all-time high, only to drop precipitously immediately after birth. So, as you go through the first few days of your postpartum journey, the following hormones will be at play:

- **Estrogen and progesterone:** Levels of these hormones will drop significantly after delivery.

- **Oxytocin:** This hormone will surge immediately after birth to make up for the body's drop in estrogen and progesterone. When you find yourself developing an intense parenting instinct during this time, just know oxytocin is the hormone responsible. But even with your new parenting instinct, this won't prevent you from going through the baby blues.

- **Prolactin:** This hormone will increase once your baby is born to encourage your body to increase its milk supply.

Changes in Breast Size, Shape, and Milk Production

After giving birth, your breasts will change, swelling and growing fuller to accommodate the increasing milk supply that's now being stored in them. For as long as you're breastfeeding your baby, your body's prolactin will work to ensure your body is producing the milk your baby needs to feed. The more your baby feeds, the more milk your body will produce.

Uterine Involution and Vaginal Discharge

After birth, your uterus will shed its thick lining. This explains your vaginal bleeding, also known as uterine involution. It's a natural process that every postpartum mother goes through, and all it does is help your body return to its prepregnancy state. After the bleeding, you'll experience a vaginal discharge, which is also known as "lochia." For the first two days, you'll notice it appearing bright red; as the days go by, it'll turn into a pink color. It will then go from pink to a light brown or yellow color.

Whether they had a a vaginal or a Cesarean birth, all women will experience vaginal bleeding and discharge. Both the bleeding and discharge will be heavy at first, with a bit of blood clotting as well, but as the weeks progress, they'll appear lighter in color.

Pelvic Floor Muscle Recovery

Pelvic floor dysfunction is common among postpartum mothers, but this shouldn't be much of a surprise: after all, you've been carrying a baby for close to 40 weeks, and experienced that baby causing numerous contractions while preparing for birth. With that in mind, it takes at least six months for your pelvic floor muscles to heal from pregnancy and birth; however, it takes about six weeks for those muscles to make significant improvements. During this time, you'll likely feel various changes, muscle functions, and sensations in your body.

Healing From Vaginal Birth

Episiotomies are used to make the vaginal opening wider when the baby is making its way out of the vagina during birth. Sometimes, women will experience tears to the perineum (the area between your rectum and vagina) as their vagina widens; therefore, episiotomies help prevent severe vaginal tears. They also help speed up the birth process so the baby comes out as fast as they need to. After birth, mothers may experience tenderness and pain as the birth process will have strained their vagina and perineum. Fortunately, it only takes a few weeks for this part of your body to heal; therefore, you don't have to worry about having your vagina and surrounding areas not return to normal after birth.

After birth, you'll still have after-birth contractions that may generate a bit of discomfort, but this is nothing to worry about; these pains are positive signs that your body is healing internally. With the contractions, your body is simply reducing all the bleeding that's happening in your uterus and shrinking your uterus back to its original size. To manage the pain and discomfort, you can invest in some of the essentials I'll be listing later in the chapter.

While recovering from your vaginal birth, it's important to ensure you take care of any stitches or tears so you reduce any chances of getting an infection. Also, heavy bleeding will require you to bathe or shower at least twice a day and to change your maternity pads as often as you can. This will help you maintain proper body hygiene, which is essential for overall physical health.

When it comes to when exactly it would be a good time to resume any form of sexual activity, health-care providers usually recommend women to wait roughly six weeks before having sex. Because of the significant hormonal changes, your vagina may feel tender and dry, especially if you happen to be breastfeeding. So, you may want to use a lubricant if you feel any discomfort during your attempt.

Recovery From Cesarean Birth

If you happen to have had a C-section, you will feel a tender pain in your lower abdomen near the incision that may go on for some days or weeks, depending on how quickly you heal; however, overall the C-section recovery process will take a little longer than the vaginal recovery process. You'll likely spend a few days in the hospital and your doctor may warn you against doing too much lifting and bending. To help with the pain, your doctor may prescribe some medication.

When it comes to caring for the scar, you should make a gentle effort to

- clean the wound at least twice a day using a mild soap, bath sponge, or washcloth

- use a clean and dry towel to dab away any excess water so it leaves the wound dry throughout the day

- wear a clean, fresh gauze bandage daily to prevent your clothes from being stained by your wound and to absorb any excess fluids or blood from your scar

After an operation, you should wait at least two weeks to engage in any kind of exercise. While you wait for those two weeks to be over, you can strengthen your abdominal muscles and support the recovery process by taking short walks around the house. Mobility can make a tremendous difference in speeding up your recovery process after a C-section. Once the two weeks are over, you can then move on to some light to moderate exercises, such as (*6 Post-Operative Abdominal Rehabilitation Exercises*, n.d.)

- pelvic tilts

- heel slides

- knee rolls

- hip lifts

- abdominal hollowing

- abdominal curl-ups

C-sections can affect you emotionally and psychologically, so it may be a good idea to consider having someone to talk to about your experience and feelings. Close friends and family who you know will provide you with the support you need would be great, but you can also reach out to a health-care professional if you're struggling with any of your emotions or suspect that your recovery may be undergoing a complication.

Managing Pain and Discomfort After Birth—Postpartum Pain and Discomfort

To address your postpartum abdominal pains and cramps, swelling breasts, sore nipples, back pain, joint aches, and muscle soreness, you can use these essentials to manage the pain and discomfort:

- medication for pain relief

- nursing pads

- a postpartum belly band

- nipple creams

- absorbent maxi pads

- cotton underwear

- a heating pad

- nursing bras

- ice packs

- hemorrhoid spray

- witch hazel pads

- a peri rinse bottle

- sitz baths

- stool softener

If you feel your pain isn't subsiding or is getting worse, please contact your doctor for medical attention immediately as this could be a serious sign of infection or another complication.

Dealing With Postpartum Body Image

Not many women are completely comfortable with their bodies after giving birth. So, as you work on embracing your new body or trying to heal it so you can lose any excess weight, here are some practical tips you can use to overcome any postpartum body struggles you may have:

- Make a habit of practicing positive affirmations.

- Express all your thoughts and feelings in a journal.

- Avoid social media as much as you can.

- Allow yourself to be present in every moment.

- Wear clothes that accommodate your current body size.

- Prepare yourself for the day before starting it.

- Avoid obsessing over how much you weigh.

- Maintain a proper diet.

- Move around as much as you can.

- Spoil yourself with beauty treatments and appointments.

- Get as much quality sleep as you can.

- Speak to a professional if needed.

Next Steps

Life after a baby will take some adjustment, but you can make it into something great for everyone. Turn to the next chapter to find out how.

Chapter Eight

LIFE AFTER BIRTH

After we got home from the hospital, I didn't shower for a week, and then John Krasinski and I were like, "Let's go out for dinner." I could last only about an hour because my boobs were exploding. When the milk first comes in, it's like a tsunami. But we went, just to prove to ourselves that we could feel normal for a second.

Emily Blunt

N avigating the "firsts" after having a baby can be a mixture of excitement, uncertainty, and learning. Understanding and preparing for these milestones and experiences can help new parents navigate the transition into parenthood with confidence and grace.

The First Days and Weeks

There's more to looking after a baby than just learning how to change a diaper, breastfeed correctly, sanitize a feeding bottle, or put a baby to sleep.

During the first few days and weeks of your newborn baby's life, everything you do will revolve around finding ways to make your new life together work. Remember that motherhood isn't just a job, it's a relationship, and for many years to come, you and your child will be working through a lot of trial and error to make your journey together a fruitful one. So, because a language barrier currently exists between you and your little one, it's up to you to establish effective routines that will help you and your baby communicate with one another properly.

How to Navigate the First Few Days at Home With a Newborn Baby

Although babies are solely dependent on us to survive, the fact that they are reliant on us while not being able to say much doesn't make caring for them any easier. This makes our daily tasks far more intense and demanding. So, between feeding your baby all day, not sleeping enough, comforting your crying baby, changing diapers, and having to keep your baby smelling clean rather than of baby puke, you'll have quite a bit on your plate during this time. But no worries—with proper guidelines on how to navigate the first few weeks, you can make the experience a little less overwhelming.

Feeding

Newborn babies drink about one to three ounces of milk at a time; however, depending on your specific baby, you may find yourself needing to feed fairly often since some babies get a little hungrier than others. While most of us believe our baby's strong cries will tell us it's time to feed them, babies can also use other cues to indicate they're hungry. This includes smacking their lips, sucking their hands, or rooting.

You want to ensure you're feeding your little one every two to three hours or so. This is because they normally lose a bit of weight within a few days of being born. Therefore, feeding your baby throughout the day and night will ensure they return to their original birth weight.

Hiccups, Baby Puke, and Burps

Many babies will puke a little after feeding. To reduce the amount of puke, it's good to burp your little one after every feed. They can do this themselves, but to control the spill and ensure they're in the right position, you may want to assist their burping process. But keep in mind that this may be a little uncomfortable for them, so don't be surprised if you notice they're a little fussy after feeding.

Soft pats and gentle circular motions are a great way to help your baby burp; avoid whacking their back as it may hurt them a little. Also, there are numerous burping positions you can explore, so try alternating between each position until you find something that will work for both of you. Should you notice your baby's regular hiccups, there's no need to panic because this doesn't cause them any discomfort. And if you notice they sometimes puke a little more or less than at other times, this is perfectly normal too. However, excessive puke may indicate your baby has reflux.

Pee and Poop

Your newborn will usually have a wet diaper between five and ten times a day, and they usually poop daily, but this will depend on whether your baby is breastfed or formula fed. During the first few weeks of birth, monitor the number of times your baby pees and poops because your doctor may ask you about this when they're checking your little one's urine and bowel movements.

Don't worry too much about the color of your baby's stool. During a newborn baby's first or second day after birth, they'll release a black stool that usually has the consistency of tar. As the days go by, their stools will be soft and turn more brown in color. However, they won't look anything close to an adult's stool; instead, they'll range between appearing seedy, greenish, yellow, light brown, or pale. Again, this will depend on whether the baby is being breastfed or formula-fed.

Crying

Everybody knows the one thing newborn babies know how to do is cry, but fortunately, your baby may be a lot quieter and more sleepy during their first few days. By now, you should have a good idea about newborn crying, what your baby could be trying to tell you, and why it's important to ensure you respond to your baby's needs each time they try to communicate those needs to you. So, to improve your experience, focus your attention on learning your baby's patterns and building a connection with them.

Sleep

Like newborn crying, we've already covered the importance of quality newborn sleep. Remember that your newborn baby will likely be asleep for about 16–18 hours a day. Track their hours to ensure they're getting enough sleep, as sleep deprivation may cause them to be a lot more restless and fussy when they're awake.

Breathing

If you find your baby breathing a little more quickly than you, then pausing, and then returning to their quick breathing, know that this is perfectly normal. However, if the breathing is accompanied by grunting, long pauses lasting longer than 15 seconds, flaring of the nostrils, heavy breathing, chest retractions, wheezing, or breathing that's fast enough to leave you concerned, it may be a good idea to speak to a doctor.

Bathing

During the first few days of your baby being home, focus on keeping your little one clean without needing to place them in a bathtub, since their umbilical cord stump may get an infection from being placed in water. Instead, you can use a damp washcloth or wipe to clean the skin.

Clothes

We've already talked about which clothing items would be best for dressing your newborn baby; however, when preparing to dress your baby, the weather and your baby's body temperature should play a crucial role in what you choose for them to wear. Because an infant's body temperature isn't the same as an adult's, you need to be a little more careful about what they wear. Generally speaking, newborn babies have body temperatures of around 99.5°F (37.5°C), which is typically higher than a child's or adult's average body temperature (*Fever*, n.d.). This is because a baby's body surface area is relatively larger in relation to their weight, and they also generate more heat because of their high metabolism. Therefore, their body temperature isn't as well-regulated as that of an older child or adult. So, each time you prepare to dress your baby, ensure you keep the season and their body temperature in mind.

When dressing your baby in warm or hot weather, ensure they wear something that's loose, light in color, and has a high UV protection factor (UPF). On very hot days, a nappy and singlet will do, but if you're planning on heading out of the house, remember to protect your baby's skin by keeping them in the shade or having them wear a sun hat. Until your baby is six months old, it's advisable not to apply any sunscreen to their skin.

During cold weather, avoid dressing your baby with thick clothing items. Instead, if you dress them in layers, you can add or remove items as the day goes on. As a rule of thumb, if you're wearing three layers of clothing, your newborn baby will need four, and if you're wearing five layers, your newborn baby will need six. Simply keep them warm by dressing them with one layer more than you're wearing—it doesn't matter where that layer goes, so it could be a vest or a cardigan.

Have you ever noticed that babies sweat the most on their heads? That's because that part of their bodies is where they lose the most heat. Since sweat cools your body temperature, it may be a good idea to place a beanie or hat on your little one's head when they're outdoors. Once home or in any type of closed setting like a mall or car, you can remove the hat to prevent overheating.

It will often cross your mind to either overdress or underdress your baby when it's seemingly too cold or too hot before bedtime. However, when preparing your little one for sleep, layer them as you would in the day and monitor their body temperature during the night when you're either feeding them or changing their diaper. During cold seasons, you may feel tempted to dress your baby in enough layers to keep them warm throughout the night; however, if your baby reaches the point of overheating, this could put them at risk of sudden unexpected death in infancy and SIDS.

So, as you prepare your baby for bedtime, work on adjusting the room's temperature so you can dress your little one comfortably. Then, when monitoring their body temperature, keep in mind that their tummies will always feel warmer than every other part of their body, while their feet and hands will generally feel a lot cooler than the rest of their body. Should your little one sweat or appear red, it may be a good idea to either reduce the number of layers they're wearing or adjust the room's temperature by cooling it down.

If you plan to swaddle your baby while they're sleeping, use thin cotton wraps or a muslin. That's because unlike blankets and other materials you can use to wrap your baby with while sleeping, thin cotton wraps and muslins don't trap body heat or limit your baby's ability to move a bit. In addition to this, the fabrics used to make these wraps are incredibly breathable and soft, since they're loosely woven and able to keep your little one calm and comfortable. The wraps also work well in mimicking the womb while keeping your baby warm, so you don't have to overdress them while they're wrapped.

If you're using a blanket, it would also be a good idea to invest in muslin or cotton fabric options. These are lightweight and perfect for any season and temperature. Like clothes, you can layer them according to how hot or cold it is at the time.

Going Out for the First Time

Going out for the first time may be a challenge because, for the most part, you carry a heavy sense of guilt, believing your little one is sitting at home waiting for you while you're out and about having the time of your life. But don't worry—these feelings of guilt are normal. Whether you like it or not, it's important for you to maintain a social life outside of your home, as this establishes a great social support circle that you'll need to help you cope throughout your new journey. Even if it means you need to find a new network of people to call friends, it's healthy to get some fresh air, indulge in your favorite activities, have a romantic date with your partner, spend some time with your friends, or find an online support group. At the end of the day, it's all about nurturing every one of your relationships so you don't lose yourself in the process of growing as a mother.

One of the biggest concerns you may have each time you plan to go out is, "Who can I trust to look after my baby while I'm away?" If you're out with your partner or can't seem to find a close friend or family member who's free to watch your baby for you, consider hiring a babysitter. These days, you can search for qualified babysitters online. Usually, agencies will list different babysitters in your area who already have a profile with the company, so you can use your specifications to find your perfect match. Once you've found someone to assist you, all that will be left to do is get ready and get going.

Baby's First Outings and Social Interactions

It's normal to sometimes need some fresh air or want to take your little one out to meet others who are close to you, like friends or family. But, because of how sensitive newborn babies are to new and unfamiliar environments, you may be wondering when would be a good time to take them out for their first outing. Fortunately, social interactions and outdoor trips are doable if your baby is healthy and up to date with their vaccinations.

During the first month after birth, it may not be a good idea to expose your little one to public spaces that are packed with people, like restaurants, stores, malls, or public transit, as these places have a lot of germs and bacteria that could cause your baby to get sick. During this period, more intimate settings would be best for any social interactions you may want to have; however, it's important to

- keep your little one away from direct sunlight

- dress your little one appropriately

- avoid places and spaces that may have insects and mosquitoes

- always keep an eye on your baby

- sanitize your hands as much as possible to keep your hands free of germs each time you handle your baby

- always pack your baby's essentials

- avoid using your stroller's handles to hang your bags

Try to also avoid taking your little one out when

- the weather is severe—cold, rain, or a storm

- the weather is exceptionally hot

- you'll be out for a long time

- your baby isn't well

Managing Public Outings and Maintaining Good Hygiene Practices

Before you or anyone else touches or handles anything that concerns your baby, it's crucial to ensure everyone has washed their hands. Using a disinfecting hand soap would be best, but hand sanitizers can work just as well, and you can always keep them close by to avoid standing at the sink each time. It's important that any hands touching your baby are kept clean at all times since the immune system of newborn babies isn't as strong as that of an older child or adult. This makes it hard for their bodies to fight off infections. By exposing them to any germs, you risk having them come in contact with all kinds of infections. Therefore, because prevention is always better than cure, keep your hands clean and ensure your baby's physical environment is also kept clean and tidy at all times. This will help prevent any accidents from happening.

When it comes to physically handling your little one, ensure that you support their head and neck at all times. This means cradling their head each time you carry them and supporting their neck when you're holding them upright or putting them down. Because a newborn's head is the largest part of their physical build, their spinal muscles are quite weak during the first few weeks of their life. This explains why they have a noticeable head lag each time you hold them upright.

When your child is a little older and able to move around on their own, firm handling and a bit of play are acceptable. However, two things you should avoid doing at all costs when you're handling or holding a newborn baby are shaking them or engaging in any rough games that involve throwing them in the air or moving their legs and knees around too much. Of course, people, including mothers, will occasionally resort to this when they wish to distract a child from doing something like crying too much. However, shaking a newborn baby can be very dangerous as it can result in your child having a bleed in the brain; if this cannot be treated, the outcome can be fatal. So, remember to remain exceptionally gentle and cautious when you're handling a newborn baby.

When you travel out in public with a newborn baby, always ensure your little one is secure. In a car, you must place your little one in a car seat to ensure they're strapped in and secure throughout the ride. Before you think of just purchasing any car seat, ensure the one you buy is suitable for newborns, as car seats are designed to support and provide comfort for children according to their weight and size. Once you're out of the car and walking around with your baby, you have the option to place your baby in a stroller or carrier. Nowadays, mothers are lucky enough to have a range of strollers to choose from, depending on their needs. However, before heading out, it can be useful to have a plan about what you intend to do so you can choose the right means of transport for your baby. If you're simply taking a walk or running an errand, a stroller can work well, but if you'll be buying groceries and carrying things around, it may be ideal to use a carrier so you can secure your baby to you throughout your time out together.

What to Remember When You're Using a Changing Table

The surface you use to change your baby may be the last thing on your mind; however, there are some points that are worth taking into consideration. "But what would I need to consider when it comes to a changing surface?" Relax—ensuring you change your baby on a surface made of diamonds and gold isn't on the agenda. Instead, it's all about ensuring that the public changing table you're using is safe and clean.

Having a newborn baby fall off a changing table is one accident no parent wants to encounter. So, it's best to change your baby on a changing table with raised edges that reach a height of about 3 inches above the surface that you've placed your baby on. For extra protection, you can also use the baby safety harness if one is provided. And remember to avoid leaving your baby unattended at all costs, even if it's "just for a second."

Introducing the Baby to Family and Friends

Preparing to introduce your little one to family and friends can be an exciting time for any mother; however, with a newborn baby, it's important to ensure your little one is handled and held safely the entire time. Newborn babies win hearts time and time again because of how tiny they are. But it's that same size that makes some people, including parents, very much afraid of physically handling and holding them. A newborn's size makes them extremely fragile and, while most people panic at the thought of dropping them accidentally, others fear holding them in positions that will make them uncomfortable.

As a first-time mom who may be keen on learning more about how to handle or hold her newborn baby, to you, holding and handling your baby means bonding with your little one so you create a safe, comfortable, and supportive space for them. However, achieving this goal can be hard to do when you're still getting a hold of everything. From time to time, experienced family and friends may step in to show you some of the best ways to connect with your baby while holding them; while this may leave you feeling you may be doing something wrong or look like you don't know what you're doing, always remember that, unless proven otherwise, those around you usually want what's best for you. So, before turning down certain suggestions, try them out in your own private time and see if it works for you.

Going Back to Work Postpartum

When your maternity leave is over, and you're just days away from heading back to work, you may start to develop a great sense of guilt. While working through your recovery and embracing your new journey, you're likely equally exhausted from all the sleepless nights, hormonal changes, and mental exhaustion. So, by the time you're heading back to work, the break you were supposed to take doesn't feel like one at all.

During this time, you may feel a great sense of anxiety, guilt, anger, excitement, and sadness simply because you're torn between leaving your baby for hours on end and returning to something that feels like "you" again. So, as you navigate through all these different emotions, you can calm yourself by

- finding your baby a childcare service that you can trust and rely on

- designing a feeding plan that you and your baby will follow

- possibly considering work opportunities that will afford you flexible hours or working from home

- taking time out for some self-care

- deep cleaning your home so you're sure your baby's in a safe and clean environment if you leave them home with a nanny

As you return to work, remember that your priorities will now have changed. Late nights at the office and going out for drinks every Friday with your colleagues may no longer be an option. So, as you return to work, keep the following adjustments in mind:

- Set some boundaries to ensure people respect your time.

- Always have a plan B when it comes to whom you choose to take care of your little one.

- Speak to HR about any parental employee benefits you may be entitled to.

- Don't allow your emotions to get the best of you.

- Redefine what you choose to make a priority.

- Exercise self-compassion.

Next Steps

New parents find that time becomes their most valuable resource—read on to find out how to make it work for you.

Chapter Nine

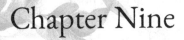

FINDING BALANCE

*There will be so many times you feel like you've failed. But in
the eyes, heart, and mind of your child, you are super mom.*

Stephanie Precourt

Effective time management is essential for new parents in the postpartum period to balance the demands of caring for a baby with their own needs and responsibilities. It involves prioritizing tasks, establishing routines, seeking support, and practicing self-care to optimize productivity and well-being.

Establishing Routines and Schedules

We establish routines and schedules to build healthy habits, keep us safe, and improve our life skills. In the process of doing so, we feel more organized and able to enjoy any free time we may have with our newborn baby. This relieves us of any stress or pressure we may face. With proper planning, we develop regular habits that train our children to become more familiar with how we do things at home, since everything is routine and predictable.

Creating a Sleeping Schedule

We've already established that a child isn't born with an already-established circadian rhythm. This explains why they're awake and asleep on and off throughout the day and night. You must allow your baby to get the hours of sleep they need at any time of the day, because, to enjoy the benefits of sleeping well from a tender age, you must ensure your little one is getting quality sleep and not just regular sleep.

Sleep isn't sleep just because you have your eyes closed. To reach the point of waking up feeling well rested and restored, you have to go through all the different sleep stages to ensure your body did all it was meant to do in getting you to rest. When we sleep, our bodies go through different sleep stages, known as rapid eye movement (REM) sleep and non-REM sleep.

REM sleep is your body's earliest stage of sleep, where you step into dreamland while your eyes move at a rapid pace. With your little one spending about 16 hours of their day sleeping, roughly 8 hours of that will be REM sleep. As your baby gets older, the time they spend in REM sleep will lessen.

Non-REM sleep is the second type of sleep and this part of your rest involves fewer eye movements, because we're now settling into a deeper stage of sleep. Unlike REM sleep, non-REM sleep is divided into four stages:

- **Stage one:** Drowsiness, where our eyes look a little droopy and open and close as we doze off.

- **Stage two:** This is a light sleep that may include a few movements and a bit of startling and jumping if we pick up on any sounds.

- **Stage three:** This is a deep sleep that involves no movement or sound from you.

- **Stage four:** This is the deepest part of your sleep.

A baby's sleep cycle will typically start with them entering stage one, moving into stages two and three, and then heading into stage four. When they're close to waking up, they'll go from stage four to three, two, and then REM. This can happen several times in a single sleep session.

When a baby is awake, they undergo different wake phases throughout the time they're engaging with you, their environment, and those around them. First, immediately after waking up, your little one steps out of their sleep cycle while remaining quiet but aware of what's happening around them. During this time, they'll remain quiet while staring at the different objects and movements around them. After some minutes, they'll move into their active stage of being alert. Here, their focus will change to objects, sounds, and movements around them that are more noticeable.

Once your little one is fully aware of their surroundings, they'll head into the crying phase, which will involve crying accompanied by erratic movements. When a baby is in their crying phase, it doesn't take much for them to "turn a pimple into a mountain." So, when you find them over-stimulated and restless, find different ways to calm the situation by lifting, singing, speaking, or swaddling them. It may take a few minutes to stop the crying, but the situation will eventually improve.

The best way to try to prevent the crying phase is to feed the baby right after waking up. This is because most mothers assume feeding the baby in their crying phase may be the solution. However, when a baby is overstimulated and moving erratically, it may be difficult to get them to calm down through feeding.

Creating a Safe and Healthy Sleep Environment

Knowing that a baby spends about half their sleeping time just closing their eyes in REM sleep should immediately encourage any parent to avoid placing a sleeping baby in a room that's filled with loud noises and distractions. It also explains why babies are quick to wake up at even the slightest sound. Each time this happens, you stop them from entering deep sleep and reduce the number of hours they have to rest.

Part of creating a healthy sleep environment means ensuring your little one rests in a dark room that's free from any natural light. Gadgets like cell phones, tablets, televisions, and laptops should also be kept out of the room as the light from these device screens can be distracting. Your baby will eventually develop their own circadian rhythm, but if you'd like to find your little one (and you!) resting well in the nighttime sooner rather than later, you may want to assist their bodies by training them how to tell the difference between day and night. By always ensuring that you put them to sleep in a dark room, their bodies will automatically work on releasing a hormone known as melatonin, which will help them fall and stay asleep once their brain is trained to signal to their body when it's dark.

When it comes to creating a safe sleep environment for your little one, this will mainly revolve around setting up a space that won't place your baby at risk of any sleep-related death like SIDS or accidental suffocation. This means

- placing your baby only on firm surfaces that won't change shape when something is placed on them

- placing your baby on a flat surface like a table when you're bathing them or changing their diaper

- ensuring your baby isn't sitting or resting at an incline

- only using a fitted sheet to cover surfaces

Avoid placing your newborn baby on an adult bed or armchair. Also, avoid leaving them alone, with young children, or with pets. If you're sitting on an armchair or couch with your baby, avoid the possibility of you falling asleep as this can be extremely dangerous.

When it comes to the surfaces you choose to place your baby on, these should always be firm, level, and flat, whether the baby is awake or asleep. At times, you may think your little one is uncomfortable if they're sleeping on a firm surface—and it's only natural to feel that, since most adults don't find any form of comfort or pleasure in sleeping or resting on a firm surface. You may mean well; however, placing your baby on a soft surface will increase the chances of them suffocating, getting strangled, or becoming a victim of SIDS. So, to prevent this, try by all means to avoid placing your little one on a

- couch

- sofa

- sheepskin

- waterbed

- blanket

- memory foam surface

- quilt

- adult mattress

Surfaces aren't the only thing you should look at, because what we cover our babies with also matters. Avoid placing your baby under any soft covering, as this also increases their chances of becoming a victim of SIDS, strangulation, or suffocation. Other points worth keeping in mind include the following:

- Avoid placing your baby on a surface that has one end higher than the other. Babies are light in weight and, because their heads are rather heavy, they can easily slide off the surface head first.

- Avoid placing your baby on surfaces like hammocks as these will elevate their feet and head while potentially blocking their airway.

- The safest option for your baby is to place them in a crib that includes nothing but a fitted sheet that covers the mattress.

- Avoid placing pillows, crib bumpers, or any sort of toy, cloth, or blanket around, under, or on top of your baby.

- Crib bedding and bumpers are known to cause a lot of serious injuries when they're placed in the same spaces as a young baby.

- Keep your baby's sleep and play environment clean and free of any clutter at all times.

- It's not advisable to turn a stroller, sitting device, or car seat into a regular sleep spot for your baby.

Strategies for Soothing a Crying Baby

When you're a first-time mom, you may wonder why your little one continues to cry despite having ensured that they are changed, fed, well-dressed, and clean. It's an age-old question that can leave you feeling highly overwhelmed, but, fortunately, it's nothing a bit of soothing can't handle. Before becoming concerned that your baby may be experiencing a great sense of discomfort or stress, your baby will most likely be crying because they're

- hungry

- feeling uncomfortable as a result of having gas trapped in their belly

- experiencing discomfort due to a wet or full diaper

- tired

- experiencing colic

- feeling bored

- overwhelmed

- too hot or cold

- sick

If your little one is still a tad fussy after ruling out all of the above points, and a health-care professional has found nothing alarming about the crying, you can always try time-tested strategies like

- swaddling

- sucking a thumb, fist, finger, or your breast

- placing your baby in a sling or front carrier

- gliding, swaying, or rocking

- white noise

- singing a song

- relaxing the baby in some warm water

- giving your baby a massage

- giving the "colic carry" a go

- spending a bit of time outside

- putting up some entertainment

Establishing a Bedtime Routine

Babies all have more or less the same required hours, but if you've noticed that your baby sleeps a little more or less than others, don't worry. What's important is to watch your little one's daily patterns and, if you notice a concerning change, habit, or behavior, you can always reach out to your pediatrician for advice.

Your baby's waking and sleeping patterns won't be the same as another baby's. With them having a sleep pattern and routine of their own, it's worth keeping in mind that your little one may not sleep during the same hours as you either. So, as you work on establishing a bedtime routine for your baby, try squeezing in some sleep as well. Otherwise, sleep deprivation will start to take a negative toll on you as you go along. Therefore, to stay healthy and active, adjust your sleep routine to accommodate your little one's sleep patterns. Plus, for the first few weeks of their life, you can always use breastfeeding as a way to help them doze off. And don't worry too much about keeping your home completely quiet during naptime; sometimes it can be good to get your little used to a little noise while sleeping.

Because babies are born without knowing any difference between day and night, you can help train their circadian rhythm by establishing a bedtime routine. Taking them out for some air during the day can do a lot of good, but ensuring your home receives a lot of natural light can also be of help. You can then keep them entertained when they're awake during the day. Noise and busyness will signal to their bodies that a lot goes on during the day, and then the calm and relaxed energy will help ease them into the night.

When the evenings arrive, set the mood for a relaxed and calm time by

- dimming the bedroom lights

- keeping noise levels down

- putting your little one to sleep immediately after they've been fed and changed

- not handling your baby too much

With a consistent routine, your baby's body will start to understand that darker settings mean nighttime has arrived and that it's time for sleep.

When it comes to where exactly your baby should sleep, your decision will depend on how much space your home has as well as your financial budget. Keeping your baby in a separate room may be great for establishing their sense of independence and space; however, to reduce the risk of SIDS, it's always advisable to either co-sleep or place your baby's cot in the same room as your own. You should try to maintain this for the first six months of their life.

Don't worry too much about establishing a bedtime routine for your newborn baby immediately after birth. During the first three months of their life, focus on creating a bond with your baby so you can establish some sort of relationship with them. Then, when your newborn hits the three-month point, you can work on introducing a bedtime routine. While you work on introducing this new routine, don't be too hard on yourself or the baby in trying to get everything to be perfect. Day by day, ease your little one into a soothing and simple routine. As you do this, give you and your little one the time you need to still have your bonding time. That way, the experience won't feel like a sleep bootcamp of some sort.

Fortunately, there's a lot you can do to help ease your baby into a bedtime routine. Instead of changing their diaper and feeding them, consider following this routine:

1. Give them a bath.

2. Dress them in a comfortable set of night clothes.

3. Put them in a fresh nappy.

4. Put them to bed.

While preparing your baby for sleep, ensure the room you're placing them in has dimmed lights. This will help to create a calm atmosphere. Then, while seated with them or putting them in their bed, consider reading them a bedtime story or singing them a sweet lullaby. Goodnight kisses and cuddles can be just as comforting. Try keeping gadgets like televisions and cell phones away from them because the screen lighting can be distracting and make it difficult for them to fall asleep. These, together with other exciting activities, can be stimulating. So, to keep your baby from struggling to fall asleep or waking up shortly after falling asleep, wind down the evening to create and maintain an atmosphere that's relaxing enough for them to fall and stay asleep.

Creating a Feeding Schedule

To create a feeding schedule for your newborn baby, you must first keep in mind that you'll be feeding your little one day and night, especially during the first few weeks after birth. This means attending to your baby's needs every two to three hours. Unfortunately, if your newborn doesn't feed this frequently, you may need to bring this to your doctor's attention. But that's about as good as it gets when it comes to establishing a feeding schedule for your baby.

When it comes to milk supply, this will adjust according to demand. The more you breastfeed your baby, the more your body will be signaled to produce more milk. If you're fortunate enough to produce an excess amount of breastmilk, instead of wasting the milk, store it by pumping it and refrigerating it after putting it into a bottle. This will also help keep your body producing more milk.

From time to time, your little one may have a series of short feeds that closely follow each other. If this happens, don't panic, because it's perfectly normal. During this cluster-feeding period, your baby is still getting the supply they need.

While breastfeeding, do all you can to stay hydrated. We've already discussed the importance of staying hydrated during your postpartum journey; try keeping a bottle of water around so you can reach for a drink each time you're seated or in the middle of a feeding session. Also, don't forget to feed yourself. We've already discussed diet plans and foods you should be focusing on. I know you may want to lose all your baby fat through a diet plan of some sort, but to keep your breastmilk nutritious, you need to eat well so you have the right energy and nutrients.

Implementing and Adjusting Your Daily Routines

You can implement a routine for any activity that you do with your newborn baby, but remember to start taking routines a lot more seriously from about three months of age. During the first three months, you want to work on your bond and connection. To do this, you'll need a lot of time and patience. Because routines require consistency and discipline, you may rush your bonding sessions to try and stick to time. For this reason, implement your routines *after* establishing your bond. These schedules can go as far as including the different play activities you'll be doing each day. And remember that, as your baby grows, it's important to adjust your schedule accordingly because their needs will certainly change.

Top New Baby Time Management Hacks

Being a postpartum mother means you hardly have time for anything and, even if you establish routines and schedules, it may sometimes be difficult to stick to them, especially when you're finally back at work. So, in an attempt to ensure you stick to your routines and schedules, here are some top time management hacks that you should apply in your everyday life:

- Prioritize every one of your tasks to figure out which is more important than the other.

- Avoid overcompensating with your child.

- Organize your home.

- Learn to say "no."

- Don't strive for perfection—just do the best you can with what you have.

- Delegate some of your responsibilities.

- Commit to your routine and make room for adjustments.

- Create a list of things you also intend to do.

- Avoid multitasking.

- Know how much time you want to spend on a task.

- Always have a backup plan for your childcare.

- Include a weekly menu in your weekly plan.

Setting Realistic Expectations

Routines and schedules will always require you to be realistic. Granted, we all want to do more and achieve increased productivity; however, routines and schedules help you establish the balance you need in your life. Therefore, this won't be possible when you're planning according to your potential and not your patterns. By setting realistic expectations, you make your routines achievable and easier to work with, but by not being realistic, you defeat the entire purpose of having a routine.

Practicing Self-Compassion

Exercising self-compassion means being kind, gentle, and understanding toward yourself whenever you make a mistake, feel you shouldn't have done something, or discover a personal weakness. Negative thought patterns usually encourage us to beat ourselves up about the past and other things we have no control over. Therefore, it's important to practice self-compassion during your postpartum journey, because this is your first time embarking on such a journey and, like everyone, you'll make many mistakes along the way. With negative thoughts and feelings, you won't be in a healthy head space to make meaningful decisions on how to change and improve certain things about yourself. But once you exercise self-compassion, your mindset and focus begin to change, because you'll magnify more of your achievements and milestones over your mistakes and failures.

Why Self-Care Is Key During Your Postpartum Journey

Motherhood is an amazing journey; however, it's also very demanding. Sadly, immediately after stepping into motherhood, many of us become so invested and occupied with the new life we've brought into this world that, before you know it, a few days will go by without you having had a decent meal, slept well, had a bath, brushed your teeth, or even combed your hair.

Ladies—once upon a time, I believed neglecting myself was acceptable and that it was the price I was paying to ensure I could be the best mother there was. I believed that depriving myself was normal and that each time I felt drained, less confident, confused, overwhelmed, and lost, it was only a sign that I was doing something right because, to me, motherhood had to look like that. To me, if I wasn't complaining about the sleepless nights, always dressing in baggy outfits, smelling like breastmilk, walking around with cracked lips, and all over the house doing one chore or the other, I wasn't doing something right. Unfortunately, this is the mentality a lot of new mothers have, because between playing superwoman and pretending to have it all together, you're gradually dying on the inside and longing for help. However, that's only because you're losing yourself while walking your motherhood journey. For now, it may seem like you're depriving and neglecting yourself to pour into your new creation, but, over time, this doesn't prove to be true.

Earlier on, I explained that your cup can be filled with either positive or negative qualities. Granted, you may regard yourself as a good person who means well and cares about others, but each time your new role as a mother demands more from you, you feel it. And even with you trying to remain strong and think of the bigger picture, the journey does eventually take a toll on you. Over time, you'll find yourself boiling with all kinds of negative thoughts and emotions; once that negativity begins to creep up on you more often than before, these qualities begin to poison your cup of good and positive qualities. Now, if what we give others is made of what our cups contain, it's only a matter of time before these negative experiences begin to affect our parenting. So, all in all, choosing to deprive, sacrifice, and neglect our needs doesn't benefit anyone. Instead, it steers us away from being the best mothers we can be.

Finding Balance

Part of finding balance means establishing boundaries and knowing when to say "no." It also means putting yourself first to afford yourself the time you need to refill your cup, so you have something meaningful to pour into those you care about. As mothers, we often lose ourselves in the process of raising our children and taking care of our families. But we need to find a balance and invest in ourselves; we're of no use to those around us when we're ill, unable to think clearly, or a mess. So, in maintaining a healthy condition across your physical, mental, and emotional health, you need to find the perfect balance for you.

Prioritizing Self-Care Activities

It's important to balance the needs of your baby with your own needs, and this is achievable through self-care. When we think of self-care, we imagine things like buying a designer handbag, soaking in a hot tub once a week, or dining at an expensive restaurant. Most times, we associate self-care with rewarding ourselves with materialistic things. I wouldn't be entirely honest with you if I didn't say that social media, celebrities, and influencers have shaped how society understands self-care. In that light, like many women, part of why we deprive ourselves of self-care is because we believe it's out of our reach since it's expensive and supported by materialistic things. It's only when you take time to truly understand what self-care is that it suddenly becomes achievable.

Essentially, self-care is a personal journey you go through to adopt behaviors, thoughts, and habits that promote health and overall wellness. So, it's anything you do to take care of your physical, mental, and emotional well-being. With that said, I'd like us to start by understanding that we're the ones in charge of defining our version of self-care. Celebrities and influencers may purchase expensive items, soak in the bathtub now and then, invest in their physical upkeep, and dine at fine-dining restaurants as part of their self-care—and that's their choice. Everyone has the right to define self-care differently, even if it means reading a book every night before bedtime, doing a fun activity every month, showering twice a day, meditating regularly, or affording yourself an indoor date night on occasion. Here, we're tasked with the job of finding what makes us happy and using those very things to invest and prioritize ourselves.

Physical Self-Care

Part of feeling good means looking good and this means making an effort to take care of your body, both inside and out. So, from eating well and staying hydrated to committing to physical exercise and dressing well, investing in your physical body is a must.

As you go about investing in your physical body, it's important to ensure you have the right mindset about everything you're doing. Because the motherhood journey is exceptionally demanding, it sometimes takes a toll on our romantic relationships. When we face any kind of rejection or disappointment from our partners, whom we'd hope would exercise patience, kindness, love, and understanding with us, this immediately undermines our self-esteem and self-confidence. We assume their attraction toward us has changed since we no longer *look* the same, thanks to the stretch marks, baby fat, slight swelling, skin changes, and more. So, many women resort to a "revenge body" plan that has them lose all the baby weight or tone their bodies, all while seemingly bouncing back when it comes to taking care of themselves.

Of course, you can always channel hurt and pain into something positive, but it's important to not find yourself making all these efforts to find validation and approval from someone else. Your efforts to invest in yourself should be for your benefit, growth, and well-being. And since you're already on the subject of connecting the condition of your physical body to how you think and feel about yourself, you should always keep in mind that your mental well-being is largely influenced by how you think and feel about yourself physically. The more effort you make to eat well, get enough rest, take your medication, attend health-care appointments, exercise, and spoil yourself, the more positive you'll feel and think about yourself.

Mental Self-Care

How you process experiences using thoughts and emotions has a significant impact on where you'll be mentally. Apart from finding joy and satisfaction in how you appear physically, it's important to pay close attention to what you feed your mind. This includes being conscious of the people and physical environments you expose yourself to.

You don't have control over the decisions other people make and how they choose to treat you. Therefore, to position your mind in a healthy and balanced way, it's good to exercise control and power over what goes on within your life. This means doing all you can to feed yourself mentally so you can keep yourself inspired, motivated, driven, willing, passionate, and enthusiastic about life.

Fortunately, unless you're dealing with underlying issues that involve a childhood trauma or mental illness, going the therapy route isn't the only option you have to work on your mental well-being. Reading, meditating, doing fun activities, taking breaks, practicing mindfulness, listening to music, tuning into your favorite podcast, reflecting on things worth being grateful for, and exercising compassion and acceptance can all work toward investing in mental self-care.

Emotional Self-Care

We sometimes use the terms "emotional" and "mental" interchangeably; however, there's a difference between the two. With mentally related topics, it's about addressing matters from a more psychological point. On the other hand, topics relating to emotions usually address the emotions and thoughts we trigger from what goes on in our mental space. This means that how we choose to take care of ourselves mentally ultimately fuels the thoughts and feelings we'll have about situations.

Encouraging someone to regulate their emotions by controlling their anger, not being quick to respond to situations hysterically, and containing their joy is far easier said than done. Because a lot goes into mastering your emotions, it can be slightly challenging to think of what exactly you can do to handle your emotions healthily and sustainably. Fortunately, it doesn't take a lot to indulge in emotional self-care because, here, the trick is to work on how to cope with uncomfortable situations.

Anger, sadness, excitement, and anxiety all come to us naturally. Unlike reading a book or going for a walk, our feelings aren't planned. Despite that, you can work on adopting coping skills that will help you address and manage the different emotions that affect those around you and sometimes leave you uncomfortable. Through emotional self-care, an intentional effort to willingly acknowledge your feelings and express yourself truthfully in a safe and regulated way can be all you need to invest in that aspect of your life.

In the event of having someone hurt your feelings or cause you to think in an unhealthy way, part of emotional self-care means being open to telling the person about how you feel so you or they can change the approach to the situation in the future. You can also include leisure activities that help you work on processing your emotions, so you're able to think and feel differently when you're placed in an uncomfortable or unfamiliar situation.

Finding and Accepting Support

Motherhood can be an incredibly heartwarming yet lonely journey. What with finding a way to "make this work," "stay true to yourself," and meet society's expectation of what being the "best mom" looks like, it's a tough and demanding journey. Knowing the daily struggles and challenges you go through as a mother, the last thing you want is to feel judged or misunderstood, even in the event of not making some of the best decisions. And it's not to say that you don't wish to be corrected—you're just exceptionally sensitive about the tone and approach that's being used to address a different matter.

Knowing how critical others can be about parenting, it can sometimes be hard to find support, even from a partner, close friends, and family. No mother ever wants to be told they're "being a bad mom," and people are slow to realize that we pick up on that even when it isn't said to us directly. So, unless you find another mom who's also gone three days without a shower, accidentally fallen asleep without switching the baby monitor on, or left the nappy on for a little too long, we choose to marinate in our "sins" instead.

Unfortunately, mom guilt is a reality for many of us. While it may seem harmless to remain quiet about certain things, entertaining thoughts about being a bad mother can affect us negatively. For this reason, it's important to have a support structure that we can rely on to vent, confirm, and be guided on many of the experiences we have as first-time moms. At the end of the day, our needs aren't just limited to worrying about whether or not we're doing great at being a mom, it's about finding support and reassurance in matters concerning

- physical and psychological changes happening within us

- our emotional needs

- the importance of having us establish a family unit

- how our self-esteem has been affected by our new journey

- struggling to communicate and stay true to our needs

With enough care and support, postpartum mothers can do well in adjusting to the change, healing, and responsibility that comes with the territory. By having a solid support network to rely on, we're able to seek help in our time of need.

Many new mothers are unable to establish a support network through friends and family. However, this isn't an excuse for you not to look to healthcare professionals or support groups for help. At the latter, you'll meet many new mothers who have the support network they need to make it through their journey, but who refuse to open up about their struggles because they feel doing so would make them appear weak. Being praised for "having it all together" is great, but remain true to yourself in all your attempts. By appearing one way while knowing you feel another on the inside, you suffer on the inside, and over time, this makes your journey dreadful, overwhelming, and exhausting.

Part of self-care means knowing your limits and asking for help when necessary. This can be very hard for many mothers to do because society often paints us as lazy or weak when we find ourselves asking for assistance. Sometimes, our independence hinders us from reaching out for help even when it's offered by those closest to us, because we fear being judged, ridiculed, or made to appear vulnerable, lazy, or weak. However, it's sometimes the trophies we long for that stop us from being the best versions of ourselves, and I'm here to tell you that there's true power in admitting when you're in need.

By simply picking up the phone to seek support, you'd be amazed at how things can truly change for you at that very moment. Being a mother to a newborn baby will have you cherish even 10 minutes of alone time, and having someone relieve you for an hour or even the whole day to have time to yourself means you can attend to any need you may have—even if that need involves you getting two hours of sleep.

Always remember that support can come in different forms. In addition to close family and friends, you have obstetric care teams, specialists, and other primary caregivers to rely on. And with you spending so much of your time at home with your baby, you can ask your support network to find different ways to be there for you so the actual journey doesn't feel lonely.

As you establish your support network, it's important to include individuals you know will be your eyes and ears. This is especially true if you or your little one are facing health complications, as it's always good to have someone who's able to spot any unusual warning signs in your corner. Yes, "mothers know best," but as a first-time mom, you need to keep in mind that this is still a learning experience for you and that having someone who's able to identify any blind spots may be a great help. At the end of the day, we're all in this together!

Feeding Schedules

Here are some quick feeding schedules you can use to establish a feeding schedule with a newborn baby who's between two and eight weeks old.

Breastfeeding

This schedule is best for babies who consume average amounts of breast milk and for moms who have average breast milk production and storage amounts.

Time	What to do
9 a.m.	Wake and feed
10 a.m.	Nap (30–60 minutes)
11 a.m.	Wake and feed
12:30 p.m.	Nap (30–60 minutes)
1:30 p.m.	Wake and feed
3:30 p.m.	Nap (30–60 minutes)
4:30 p.m.	Wake and feed
6 p.m.	Nap (30–60 minutes)
6:30 p.m.	Wake and feed
7:30 p.m.	Catnap (20–30 minutes)
8 p.m.	Wake and feed
9:30 p.m.	Catnap (20–30 minutes)
10 p.m.	Wake and feed
11:30 p.m.	Feed and bedtime
3:30 a.m.	Feed and right back to sleep
6:30 a.m.	Feed and right back to sleep

Babies who eat smaller amounts, babies with reflux, and moms who produce and store smaller amounts of breastmilk will need a different schedule. These babies will tend to eat more often throughout the day. Babies who eat larger amounts per feed and moms who produce and store greater amounts of breast milk will feed less often than average babies.

Formula Feeding

This schedule suggests longer naps and fewer feedings than the breastfeeding schedule above, simply because formula is more difficult for the baby to digest. So, babies tend to feel fuller for longer and therefore need slightly fewer feedings.

Time	What to do
9 a.m.	Wake and feed
10 a.m.	Nap (60–90 minutes)
11:30 a.m.	Wake
12:30 p.m.	Feed and nap (30–60 minutes)
1:30 p.m.	Wake
3 p.m.	Feed and nap (60–90 minutes)
4:30 p.m.	Wake and feed
6 p.m.	Nap (30–60 minutes)
6:30 p.m.	Wake
7:30 p.m.	Feed and nap (30–60 minutes)
8:30 p.m.	Wake
9:30 p.m.	Nap (30–60 minutes)
10 p.m.	Wake and feed
11:30 p.m.	Feed and bedtime
4:30 a.m.	Feed and right back to sleep
7:30 a.m.	Feed and right back to sleep

Next Steps

In the end, you can lose yourself for a while with all the new demands of your postpartum, but it's vital to maintain a sense of self as much as possible for your own mental health. We'll explore how you can do this in the final chapter of the book.

Chapter Ten

FINDING YOURSELF

Having kids is wonderful, and life-changing, and rarely what you're prepared for. I love my children more than anything in the world. But like a lot of women, I too struggled with postpartum depression after my first baby was born. I got help and made it through, and every day since has been the best gift I could ever have asked for. To those of you going through this, know that you're not alone and that it does get better.

Sarah Michelle Gellar

I've come across many moms who've invested so much of themselves in their children and homes that they completely lose sight of who they are outside of those roles. Before becoming a mom, I somehow believed this was deliberate, because I could never understand how an adult who's old enough to be a parent could consciously give so much of themselves to a role without realizing they're in danger of no longer recognizing who they are. After becoming a mom, I realized that giving ourselves up is an effortless and selfless thing we do as mothers, because we're devoted to ensuring we do our best to raise our children the right way while offering them memorable experiences that many of us wish we could have had ourselves.

While it's beautiful to realize the gift you have to give life and how much of an impact you have on an individual, you need to remember you still have your own life, relationships, and commitments to attend to as well. While some may see their life outside of being a mother as a distraction, finding and maintaining your own identity gives your postpartum journey more meaning. It also helps you get the support you need from those closest to you, because you will allow yourself to nurture other relationships outside of your home. Therefore, making a sacrifice to be the best mother you can be shouldn't come at the expense of your identity.

Shifting Self-Identity

Because motherhood is a life-changing experience, it somehow forces you to change your identity. As you work on crafting this new person, you will be very vulnerable and delicate, because societal expectations and cultural influences often have a part to play in shaping this new person you're becoming. Unlike PPD and the other mental illnesses some postpartum moms face, every mother goes through this period of reshaping their identity. Depending on where you are mentally, this could either make you more or less like yourself.

We often spend a lot of time on social media, and, because the internet gives rise to things like mom-shaming, you may develop a great sense of fear that you are the bad mom that everybody dislikes. For this reason, you may try everything in your power to meet the virtual standards of being a "perfect mother," but in the process of doing so, you lose yourself because you're made to believe you're a bad mother for putting yourself first. So, when you build a picture of what losing your identity as a mom looks like, you see that being the perfect mom is

- not committing to your basic needs consistently

- putting everything you desire and enjoy on hold

- no longer nurturing any personal relationships you may have

- not giving your partner the attention they desire because your children now come first

Rediscovering and Redefining Your Identity

Embracing your new role as a mother doesn't mean you now have to shut yourself off from the world and neglect your personal needs. You can still be the mother you want to be while ensuring you're also cared for in the process, because motherhood isn't meant to be a punishment. It's a beautiful experience that's meant to bring you joy and growth amid all the changes and challenges you'll be going through. Therefore, in rediscovering and redefining yourself, you need to reflect on your values, interests, and passions. You'll also have to look at identifying your strengths, talents, and personal aspirations. In this way, you'll nurture your growth and your process of self-discovery. Thankfully, there are ways in which you can still be the mom you want to be while ensuring you don't lose yourself in the process:

- Replace all the things you "should" be doing with the things that you "want" and "need" to be doing.

- Avoid spreading yourself thin all the time or always trying to "do it all."

- Get the support you need from the very beginning.

- Dedicate a lot more time to yourself.

Navigating Relationships and Social Roles

Motherhood will require you to spend a lot more time with your baby because your and their needs will always come first on your list of priorities. But as you do this, don't forget to nurture other relationships within your social circle. Yes, you may no longer be able to go out the way you used to, spend a whole two hours on the phone, or just be spontaneous for the day, but that much-needed effort you make to attend special functions, do a wellness check, celebrate milestones, and be a shoulder to cry on during difficult times can be all your partner, family, and friends need at the time. All this needs is just a little balance and planning.

With boundaries, manageable and healthy expectations, and communication, you can still balance the various roles you play in your personal life. It's simply about committing to the process while ensuring your social circle is made up of people who respect and understand your new role.

Embracing Growth and Your Evolving Identity

Having an identity doesn't mean remaining stuck in the old you. It means you're embracing this new chapter of your life to grow and evolve in the process of becoming a new individual. The postpartum journey may be challenging to get through, but there's a lot you can take from the experience in terms of learning your strengths and discovering a few of your shortcomings and weaknesses. It's all part of your personal development, because it gives you the platform to discover and reflect more on yourself. Therefore, with the right mindset, this experience can turn out to be an ever-growing one filled with lots of love, acceptance, learning, and change. As you grow through what you're going through, I encourage you to put every experience, thought, emotion, milestone, and lesson in a journal to document your journey. One day, you'll witness your child become this influential and whole individual and, when this happens, return to your journals to remember where they come from and see how far you've both come from there.

CONCLUSION

Now you've reached the end of this book, it's pretty clear that the postpartum journey isn't just about mood swings, the "baby blues," losing weight, and complaining about your stretch marks. From various mental illnesses and struggling with mom guilt to understanding baby cues and learning how to bond with your newborn, this is a journey that requires a lot of patience, understanding, and self-compassion. In the process of you learning about this little person you've given life to, you also come to discover a lot about yourself, and this grows you as an individual. With practical tips on how to navigate through common postpartum experiences, attend to your newborn baby's needs in the best way possible, and prepare for the journey ahead, you now have the "how" to every one of your questions.

With every lesson and experience I've shared with you so far, I want you to know that I can confidently stand and tell you that by applying each of these steps and techniques in my postpartum journey, I've seen tremendous growth and change in my life. So, I can only wish the same for you as you journey ahead. As you embark on this transformative journey of postpartum motherhood, remember that you aren't alone. The challenges, joys, and complexities that come with this incredible phase of life are shared by countless women around the world. Let this book be your guide, your companion, and your source of inspiration as you navigate the joys and challenges of postpartum motherhood. It's time to reclaim your power, redefine your identity, and embrace the incredible woman and mother you have become. You are capable. You are resilient. You are enough.

If you feel that this book has changed your whole outlook on your postpartum journey, please leave a positive review wherever you buy your books so someone else can also be inspired to do the same. Wishing you an amazing journey ahead!

GLOSSARY

- **Acceptance and commitment therapy (ACT):** A form of psychotherapy that branches into analyzing clinical behavior.

- **Adhesive bandage:** A plaster.

- **Aerobic exercise:** Physical exercise that increases your heart rate.

- **Antibiotic ointment:** Medication applied on the top layer of the skin to kill any bacteria present.

- **Areola:** The small pigmented circular area surrounding the nipple.

- **Baby blues:** Negative emotions that occur within the first few days of giving birth.

- **Biodegradable:** A substance or object that can decompose thanks to the action of a living organism or bacteria.

- **Bowel movement:** The movement of feces following the process of digestion

- **CBT-I practitioner:** A trained professional in cognitive behavioral therapy for insomnia (CBT-I) who helps patients identify thoughts, behaviors, and emotions that contribute to symptoms relating to insomnia.

- **Circadian rhythm:** The 24-hour internal clock that your body uses to regulate cycles of being awake and asleep by responding to environmental changes in light.

- **Cluster feeding:** Times when a baby requires short feeds every few hours.

- **Colic:** Severe pain and discomfort in a baby's abdomen caused by an obstruction of wind.

- **Cortisol:** A primary stress hormone.

- **C-section:** A surgical procedure formally known as a Cesarean section where one or more babies is born through an incision made in the mother's abdomen.

- **Dermatitis:** A condition that causes irritation and swelling in the skin.

- **Eco-friendly:** Something that doesn't affect or harm the environment.

- **Episiotomy:** A surgical incision between the anus and vaginal opening during childbirth.

- **Estrogen:** A hormone that develops and regulates the female reproductive system.

- **Internal clock:** A bodily system that controls different actions like eating and sleeping.

- **Lactating:** The process a woman's body undergoes in making and secreting breast milk.

- **Latching:** How a baby fastens on a woman's breast during breastfeeding.

- **Lochia:** Discharge from the uterus of a woman after childbirth.

- **Leaky gut syndrome:** A speculative condition presenting various digestive issues like diarrhea, bloating, and abdominal discomfort.

- **Melatonin:** A hormone that helps regulate your circadian rhythm.

- **Muslin:** A lightweight cotton cloth.

- **Newborn attachment theory:** A theory that focuses on the relationship between mothers and their newborn babies.

- **Non-rapid eye movement (REM):** A stage of sleep that work to quieten and slow down the brain.

- **Obsessive compulsive disorder (OCD):** A personality disorder that's characterized by an excessive need to attain perfection, orderliness, control, and attention to detail.

- **Obstructive sleep apnea (OSA):** An airway blockage that prevents air from traveling through your windpipe.

- **Oxytocin:** A hormone that stimulates contractions during labor and lactation after giving birth.

- **Perineal tears:** When the skin and soft tissue of a woman's vagina separate from the anus.

- **Peripartum depression:** Depression that begins during pregnancy.

- **Polyunsaturated fats:** Fat molecules consisting of more than one carbon bond that's unsaturated in the molecule.

- **Postpartum depression:** A depressive mental illness that goes beyond the typical "baby blues" after the birth of a baby

- **Postpartum panic disorder:** A postpartum depressive state that's accompanied by excessive worry, anxiety, and panic.

- **Postpartum post-traumatic stress disorder (PTSD):** A stress disorder that occurs due to a traumatic event that took place during the birth of a baby.

- **Postpartum psychosis:** A medical condition that disrupts a mother's sense of reality after delivering her baby.

- **Progesterone:** A hormone that regulates female menstruation and maintains pregnancy.

- **Prolactin:** A hormone that helps mothers produce milk after childbirth.

- **Reflux:** A digestive disease that causes an individual's stomach acid to irritate their food pipe lining.

- **Rapid eye movement (REM):** A sleep stage accompanied by various eyeball movements while someone is dreaming.

- **Restless leg syndrome:** A condition that makes an individual's legs move uncontrollably.

- **Sudden unexpected death in infants (SUDI):** An unexplained death that occurs in a child who's no more than a year old.

- **Sudden infant death syndrome (SIDS):** An unexplained death that occurs in a child who's no more than a year old.

- **Suprachiasmatic nucleus (SCN):** A part of the human brain that regulates your circadian rhythm.

- **Swaddling:** A practice of wrapping an infant in a cloth or blanket to restrict limb movements.

- **Thyroid hormone:** A hormone that controls your metabolism.

- **Thyroid gland:** A part of the body responsible for producing and secreting various hormones in the body.

- **Uterine involution:** The process by which a woman's uterus returns to its prepregnancy state.

- **Urinary tract infection (UTI):** An infection that takes place in the urethra, bladder, or kidneys.

- **UV protection factor (UPF):** How much UV radiation a fabric will allow to reach the skin.

- **White noise:** Soothing sound distractions that block environmental noises.

REFERENCES

Allison. (n.d.). *Tips for staying hydrated while pregnant and breast-feeding*. Happy Family Organics. https://www.happyfamilyorganics.com/learning-center/article/practical-tips-for-staying-hydrated/

Babhakan, J. (2022, March 30). *9 myths new moms should stop believing ASAP*. The Healthy.

Baby blues after pregnancy. (n.d.) March of Dimes.

The basics of postpartum panic disorder. (2023, July 23). Postpartum Depression.

Bastos, F. (2022, July 7). *Why you're not your thoughts: How to stop identifying with mental suffering*. MindOwl.

Betz, M. (2022, September 14). What is self-awareness and how to develop it. BetterUp.

Bhati, K. (2023, March 10). *"I need help!" How to ask for emotional support?* CalmSage.

Bonding and attachment. (2019, December 13). Caring for Children.

Bonding myths. (2018, March 10). Adoption in Child Time.

Bottle feeding advice. (2023, September 22). National Health Service.

Brusie, C (2020, April 27). *An overview of feeding your baby.* Verywell Family.

Centers for Disease Control and Prevention. (2023a, March 21). *Newborn breastfeeding basics.* https://www.cdc.gov/nutrition/infantandtoddlernutrition/breastfeeding/newborn-breastfeeding-basics.html

Centers for Disease Control and Prevention. (2023b, May 19). *Infant formula preparation and storage.*

CHOC. (2022, January 18). *Easy tips for grooming your newborn.*

Costello, H. (n.d.). *You are not alone. Sharing our stories of hope and healing.* Postpartum Resource Center of New York.

Crane, D. (Writer), Kaufmann, M. (writer), Klein, D. (Writer), & Epps, S. (Director). (2002, October 3). The one where Emma cries [TV series episode]. In Bright, K., Cohen, T., Crane, D., Goldberg-Meehan, S., Kaufmann, M., Reich, A., & Silveri, S. (Executive Producers), *Friends.* Bright/Kaufmann/Crane Productions; Warner Bros. Studios.

Davis, J. L. (2008, August 7). *What baby skin care products does your newborn need?* WebMD.

Eatough, E. (2022a, January 10). *The hidden struggle of working moms? Guilt. Here's how to overcome it.* BetterUp.

Eatough, E. (2022b, August 18). *Here's how identifying your stress triggers can help you to relax.* BetterUp.

Emotions quotes. (n.d.). BrainyQuote.

Emotional & social development in babies: Birth to 3 months. (2023, July 18). healthychildren.,org, American Academy of Pediatrics.

Facts about postpartum depression. (n.d.). Illinois Department of Public Health.

Felton, K. (2023, September 15). *The best bottles for breastfed babies, according to nursing moms.* What to Expect.

Fever. (n.d.). Penn Medicine.

Fields, S. (2016, August 31). *8 warning signs of postpartum depression.* WebMD.

From wide-awake to fast-asleep: Baby's sleep patterns. (n.d.). Nationwide Children's.

Funny Bear. (2023, May 11). *Why are cotton clothes best for baby clothes?* [Image attached] [Post]. LinkedIn.

Glover, A. (2023, September). *5 reasons why you need a postpartum support network.* American College of Obstetricians and Gynecologists.

Gold, C. (2022, July 18). *Postpartum body image struggles? 12 tips to help find peace.* Hello Postpartum.

Gordon, K. (2021, September 26). *35 honest postpartum experiences shared by real moms.* Verywell Family.

A guide for first-time parents. (2023, May 1). Nemours Kids Health.

Hadel, C. (2020, July 27). *10 mommy myths.* Associated Physicians.

Harnish, A. (2023, February 1). *What I wish someone told me about pelvic floor recovery before I gave birth.* What to Expect.

Harris, W. C. (2023, June 28). *The best way to sleep after giving birth.* Parents.

Helping your baby to sleep. (2023, May 18). National Health Service.

Hempsey, A. (2021, March 20). *Feel like you're losing your identity in motherhood? Read this.* Hello Postpartum.

Hill, C. (2023, July 13). *6 tips to maintain your mental health after baby.* Intermountain Health.

How much milk your baby needs. (n.d.). WIC Breastfeeding Support, U.S. Department of Agriculture.

How to ease common postpartum digestive issues. (2021, March 3). Mother Nutrient.

How to know when your baby's ready for sleep. (2023, May 3). Cradlewise.

Huysamen, L. (2022, February 20). *5 tips for choosing baby clothes for the first year.* Kaboutjie.

Kangaroo care (n.d.). Cleveland Clinic.

Keeping hydrated during pregnancy and the postpartum period. (n.d.). Storkhelpers.

Kleidon, A. K. (2022, October 28). *15 myths about being a new mum.* Project Hot Mess.

Kotlen, M. (2021, July 16). *The basics of breastfeeding: Everything you need to know to get started.* Verywell Family.

Lebow, H. I. (2021, July 16). *How to replace negative thoughts.* PsychCentral.

Lindberg, S. (2020, January 27). *The best postpartum exercises to do right now.* H. (2020, January 27). Healthline.

Louis, A. (2020, December 7). *Promoting healthy attachments with children.* HiMama Early Education Blog.

Lopez-Gonzalez, D. M., & Kopparapu, A. K. (2022). *Postpartum care of the new mother.* StatPearls Publishing.

Marie, K. (2023, August 23). *Newborn feeding schedule (from birth to 2 weeks): Amounts, food chart and more.* (n.d.). Huckleberry.

Mayo Clinic. (2022a, July 1). *Diaper rash.*

Mayo Clinic. (2022b, November 4). *Postpartum depression.*

McCallum, K. (2021, February 17). *Postpartum exercise: What to know about exercising after pregnancy.* Houston Methodist.

Mcleod, S. (2023, August 16). *Attachment theory in psychology.* Simply Psychology.

McSweeney, M. (2023, March 3). *Postpartum digestive issues? What you can do to help your gut.* Hello Postpartum.

Migala, J. (2023, August 18). *8 permanent body changes after pregnancy.* Health.

Mindfulness definition: What is mindfulness? (2020, February 6). YouMatter.

Nair, A. (2019, March 12). *Time management – 12 tricks for parents to stay on track.* Parenting FirstCry.

National Institute of General Medical Sciences. (2023, August 15). *Circadian rhythms.*

Nguyen, H. (2023, March 27). *What to expect after giving birth and the postpartum recovery process.* Health Partners.

Nikolopoulou, K. (2023, February 2). *What is negativity bias? | Definition & examples.* Scribbr.

ParentCo. (2021, May 7). *The link between emotional eating and parenthood.*

Parenting a newborn: Taking care of yourself. (n.d.). Healthy Parents Healthy Children.

Pelham, V. (2023, May 2). *The difference between postpartum anxiety, OCD and psychosis.* (n.d.). Cedars-Sinai. l

Perry, C. (2022, July 1). *When can newborns go outside?* The Bump.

Perry, C. (2023, June 2). *What to expect with postpartum hormone changes.* Parents.

Phillips, H. (2022, April 8). *What causes postpartum insomnia? And how to get rest.* Verywell Family.

Postpartum depression. (n.d.). March of Dimes.

Postpartum depression types. (2023, June 23). Postpartum Depression.

Postpartum intrusive thoughts: Managing mental health in early motherhood. (2021, November 9). UPMC Health Beat.

Postpartum post-traumatic stress disorder. (2021, September 24). Postpartum Support International.

Ragland, L. (n.d.). *Ways to manage stress.* WebMD.

Riley, L., Sinrich, J., & Harris, N. (2023, August 24). *How to ease into a postpartum exercise routine after birth*. Parents.

Safe sleep environment for baby. (n.d.). Safe to Sleep.

Self-care. (n.d.). University of Toledo.

Souza, K. (2022, September 23). *Comforting postpartum depression quotes for 2022*. Choosing Therapy.

Scott, E. (2023, February 13). *5 self-care practices for every area of your life*. Verywell Mind.

6 post-operative abdominal rehabilitation exercises. (n.d.). Performance Health.

Sheppard, S. (2023, April 26). *Physical touch as a love language: What it means*. Verywell Mind.

Shirong, C. (2020, June 19). *Why is sleep so important to babies?* Agency for Science, Technology, and Research, Singapore Institute for Clinical Sciences.

Skin-to-skin contact. (2023, January 7). Unicef.

Sleep/wake cycles. (n.d.). Johns Hopkins Medicine.

Stacy. (2019, February 27). *Why eye contact is important in communication*. Brandastic.

Stanborough, R. J., & Lee, M. (2023, September 20). *How to find a therapist: 8 tips for the right fit*. Healthline.

Stuck on negative thinking. (n.d.). Care Counseling.

Tips for keeping infants and toddlers safe: A developmental guide for home visitors – young infants. (2023, June 23). Early Childhood Learning &

Knowledge Center.

Traxler, C. (2023, April 14). *Postpartum diet plan: Best foods to eat after giving birth*. Zaya.

Typical sleep behaviour (1) – newborns 0 to 3 months. (n.d.). Better Health Channel.

Understanding Newborn Behaviour. (n.d.). Physiopedia.

Waters, S. (2021, May 27). *Advice on going back to work after maternity leave*. BetterUp.

Webster, R. (2023, June 22). *A social life after baby? Yes!* ZERO to THREE.

Wold, S. (2023, March 6). *Emotional challenges of motherhood*. Thought Partners.

Made in the USA
Las Vegas, NV
15 December 2023

82854188R00115